REVISED EDITION

STEPHEN
SCANNIELLO

A YEAR OF

ROSES

COOL SPRINGS PRESS
A Division of Thomas Nelson Publishers
*Since 1798*

# DEDICATION

*To Dana, always.*

Published by Cool Springs Press
a Division of Thomas Nelson, Inc.,
P. O. Box 141000
Nashville, Tennessee, 37214

Cataloging in Publication information is available.
ISBN: 1591862485

First printing 2006
Printed in the United States of America
10 9 8 7 6 5 4 3 2 1

Cover Design by Surface Works Design
Illustrations by Elayne Sears
Typesetting by S.E. Anderson

Cool Springs Press books may be purchased in bulk
for educational, business, fundraising, or sales
promotional use. For information, please email
**SpecialMarkets@ThomasNelson.com**.

Visit the Thomas Nelson website at
**www.ThomasNelson.com** and the Cool Springs Press
website at **www.coolspringspress.net**

# PREFACE

Nine seasons of roses have passed since the first publication of this book, and eight since I left the Cranford Rose Garden to pursue a career of fretting over other people's black spot and mildew. I also have my *own* rose pests now, as Dana and I now have a house and garden in southern New Jersey. This has been a big step for us from our original stoop garden of one container in Brooklyn.

In the world of roses not much has changed in nine years, except perhaps the way we approach rose gardening. There has been some exciting progress with safer techniques in the efforts to control diseases and pests among our favorite flower. Perhaps the most exciting news lately is the creation of a new group of roses known as Earthkind roses. This is an eclectic collection of cultivars, some new and some old, being tested and evaluated throughout the country for cold hardiness and pest resistance. In this group you'll find old favorites such as 'Mutabilis' and 'Distant Drums', as well as new hybrids bred from a gene pool of roses with a strong resistance to diseases. I discuss these roses in this book, as I am myself, just learning about this program.

Japanese beetles, black spot, thrips, midge, and mildew—all pests of roses I discussed nine years ago, are still here. I even came across a few more to make life more interesting and challenging in the rose garden. Progress has been made in banishing dangerous chemicals and improving the effectiveness of more environmentally sound pest management techniques. That's all in this book. New miracle solutions for growing perfect roses continue to come and go, but nothing really beats good old fashioned manure and manure tea. I still recommend that. I have become enamored with new organic fertilizers that are a combination of fish emulsion and seaweed. With the best fragrance of both ingredients, as well as the nutrient punch, what else could a rosarian ask for!

Serious rose exhibitors still build elaborate contraptions to protect their roses from the elements. New cultivars continue to come out every spring inspiring dreams of blue ribbons at the local rose show as well as perfect roses in the garden. As new "fads" are introduced annually (they're still trying to create a true blue rose!), the rose nursery catalogs are as slick as ever. In the world of old roses, the name discrepancies continue, the arguments still persist. This time, I throw in my two cents in regard to an old favorite of mine, "MacGregor's Damask". Let the games begin!

I have corrected myself, too. For instance, it's the Minnesota "Tip", *not* the Minnesota "Dip"—my apologies to the Minnesota Rose Society. I still feel the sting of being pelted with manure for that error! I do hope that my gardening friends in the twin cities will forgive me, and I still give them the highest marks for all that work they endure for the love of a rose!

I return to the Cranford Rose Garden often and it still inspires me. I enjoy the solitude of this garden in the winter as well as the madness of the June bloom. I do confess, however, that in August, I'd rather be at the beach. My volunteers are still there, though my very first one, Ruth, is no longer with us but her favorite rose, 'Harison's Yellow' is. It's under this shrub that she discovered and coveted the viola seedlings that blew in from the nearby compost pile. Izzy and Norma are no longer with us as well, but the memory of their battle over hip height still remains as fresh as the day they started cutting the roses back in December, many years ago. Bob has retired, but Sue, Marianne, Rich, Dagni, and Ruth #2 are still there pruning, planting, tying, kvetching, and watching over the collection with loving and stern eyes as a succession of new rosarians have come and gone thru the garden gate to tend this magnificent collection.

Some of my favorite roses are gone as well—removed in the name of progress, or so they say. 'Clytemnestra' no longer graces the rose arc pool, 'Knockout' now explodes into a red display in its place. 'Curly Pink' has been banished from this area as well; they still haven't found anything that could replace the beautiful display of this hybrid tea. The hill side garden is thriving and the now mature Red-tailed hawk still has rabbits for dinner. The maple trees that stole nutrients from my old rose border along the east side during my entire tenure as curator are now gone. No, I had nothing to do with that. Old age took them, too. Now, the old garden roses in the east border are flourishing under the watchful eye and excellent care of Anne O'Neill the current, and extremely dedicated, rosarian and curator.

In my own garden, among the numerous varieties of roses, I grow 'Clytemnestra' and 'Harison's Yellow', as well as a collection of polyanthas given to me from my volunteers. These roses were all grown from cuttings taken from the Cranford collection. Since I share this garden with Dana, it's only fair that I grow his favorite plants as well. After years of growing just roses in the botanic garden, I now have the opportunity to explore rose companions, and I'm hooked. I wouldn't grow roses any other way. This has been a major change of gardening style for me and I'm happy to share this with you in this new edition of *A Year of Roses*. Maybe I can convince you to grow your roses in a similar fashion?

Over the last nine years, I've seen some of my enthusiasm for roses rub off on my family members. My niece, Laura, now works full time with me tending our clients' roses with loving care. Carla and Oriana have each spent time in the gardens. Billy thinks he can grow roses in the shade. My sister Cris (Laura's mother) has mastered the art of growing roses in the red clay soil of Whitehall, Pennsylvania. My nephew Eric has become a rose rustler. The rambler taking over my brother's garden in Boulder, Colorado was grown from a cutting Eric pocketed out of my Barnegat garden during one of their fishing trips. And in Barnegat, Mom is still trying to outsmart the deer, though she's more willing these days to share some of her roses with them.

I continue to plant and prune roses all over the country in gardens of all sizes. From Maine to Texas; in the sandy loam of eastern Long Island to the thick, impenetrable clay of Virginia, the gooey gumbo soil of New Orleans, and in dusty gardens of Colorado and Arizona. These gardens, our garden in Barnegat, and forever, the Cranford Rose Garden, are the sources of the information that fills this book.

Join me, once again, as I slip on my favorite gloves and head to the rose garden. We've got lots of work to do!

# ACKNOWLEDGMENTS

*Angela Miller*

*Ramona Wilkes*

*Elayne Sears*

*Lola Honeybone*

*Cindy Games*

*Hank McBride*


*. . . Thank you*

# CONTENTS

# JANUARY

It was in January that I learned the truth about roses. Their beauty is unsurpassed, even in the deepest midwinter.

As I slide or crunch past the rose garden, I can see a carmine glow in the distance that lures me in through the gates. Although the rosebushes are dormant and the garden is buried with snow, the myriad colors and textures create a garden of interest, deserving a closer inspection even during the coldest month of the year.

I pass under the tall arching, purple-red canes of *Rosa glauca* as I venture among the snow-covered beds. There are features of certain roses—all but lost when the garden is in full bloom—that will strongly attract the eye at this time of year. What initially caught my attention are the intense colors of the naked stems; in this case my sighting is a dense planting of two North American native roses, *Rosa arkansana* and *Rosa setigera*.

Rose stems—or canes—vary from rich plum colors, such as those of our native 'Prairie Rose' and many of the gallica and damask classes, to the dusty green coloring of *Rosa davurica*, a Chinese native. There are colorful canes everywhere, even among the less attractive forms of the hybrid teas and floribundas. But the most unusual sighting of all is the peeling bark of the 'Chestnut Rose', also known as the 'Burr Rose' down south. This reminds me more of a sycamore tree than a rose, as the older, gnarled canes have layer upon layer of curling bark.

Rose hips of every shape and size (the apple-like berries containing the seeds of roses) are the colorful reminders of flowers now long gone. Hanging over the walkways from canes trained to arches are the large pumpkin-colored hips of the climbing roses 'City of York' and 'Complicata', as well as clusters of orange-red hips from 'Seagull'.

Meanwhile, all around me, the hips from shrub roses such as 'Carefree Beauty', 'Coral Creeper', and 'Trigintipetala' are being enjoyed by the winter residents of the garden. Darting back and forth across the paths are squirrels hastily foraging the fruits of the roses. Winter birds such as slate-colored juncos and cardinals are feasting on the softer hips of the rugosa roses.

This beauty of the winter rose garden, something every rosarian ought to cherish as much as the first flush of spring roses, is an experience that can be yours, too. From the moment you plant your first rose bush *you* are a rosarian.

If you're just starting with roses, this is as good a time as any to become acquainted with the local rose society. Many of these groups post meeting announcements in libraries or in daily newspapers. Get to know some of your neighboring rosarians. But let me warn you, they can be an opinionated bunch. Some hate old roses, others hate hybrid teas, some grow *only* miniatures, and then there are the rose exhibitors. But more about this breed of rosarian in **June**.

Rose society members take their roses seriously (maybe a little bit too much so), but they all have one thing in common: the love of roses and the willingness to share their knowledge. And if you're a fan of mystery novels, why curl up with a book? You'll soon find that rose societies are full of adventure, and their meetings full of intrigue.

It was in January that I became a rosarian. Until then, January was a month of rest; a time for winter vacation. But not now—there's work to be done! Now's the time to finish (or start) putting together rose orders; to find the right source for that perfect rose.

January is a good time to order roses, whether you are in the warm south or the frigid north. It's very unlikely in January that you'll find any roses at your local nursery. You can wait until they start stocking up in the spring, or you can order them yourself through the mail.

Ordering roses from a catalog is really easy. If you haven't done this before, you'll discover as I did that catalogs will expose you to varieties you would never see at a local garden center. This is a perk of mail-order roses.

If you're lucky enough not to have a mailbox stuffed with catalogs (by now mine is overflowing, including ones from nurseries I've never even dealt with) you can go to the local rose society, public library, botanic garden, or horticultural society to find the most current rose nursery catalogs. **Now that ordering on the internet has become common, most rose nurseries now offer online catalogs complete with color illustrations of their roses. I suppose it's only a matter of time before you can push a button and smell these beauties, as well!**

There are over 100 nurseries from Canada to Florida that specialize in mail-order roses. Some feature old garden roses exclusively, some sell only modern roses, and many offer a wide variety of both old and new. You might be reluctant to order from Texas if you live in Maine, or perhaps you feel that a northern nursery doesn't know beans about the arid conditions of Arizona. As long as you don't pick a rose variety that's not suited for your climate, it doesn't really matter where the rose was raised. Roses can acclimate themselves readily from one environment to another.

Rose catalogs are various in style and quality, from glossy color booklets to simple black-and-white sheets. Color catalogs offer you the advantage of seeing photos of the roses. But don't be put off by a catalog that looks like local school children put it together. Some of the best roses to be found anywhere may be listed on those stapled, black and white pages.

I immediately recycle catalogs that praise the wonders of the climbing blue roses. (There aren't any true blue roses!) Likewise the ones that boast of survival in the deepest freezes and hottest droughts, or claim that their roses will indeed bloom in the shade. This is just the perpetual fiction of the mail-order business.

I purchase nearly 95 percent of my roses from catalogs. The quality of the plants is superb, and I find that my dollar stretches far.

To get the best satisfaction when ordering, I have found it's helpful to be familiar with the different ways roses are prepared and shipped to your garden.

Every rose nursery should provide the following information somewhere in their catalog:

- How the roses are propagated
- Are the roses budded or own-root?
- How the roses are shipped (bare-root or in pots?)
- When the roses are shipped
- What time of year?
- When the roses are dormant or growing?

If you don't find this information, be sure to call the nursery before you send in an order. It's in your interest to know the answers. Get to know your sources.

One of the longest-running disagreements among rose experts is which type of rose plant is best: an **own-root rosebush** or a **budded rosebush**. There's no right or wrong answer to this. Both styles produce healthy plants. Which one is best for you depends on where you garden, and sometimes on the actual variety you've chosen.

Over the years, I've discovered that certain hybrid teas on their own roots won't have the same vigor as a budded plant of the same variety. This is true for many rose classes. But gardeners who live where the summers are very hot, or where the winters are very cold, will eventually find that the best roses for them are those that are not budded, but grown on their own root system. In my climate in Brooklyn, and in the majority of the United States, both styles grow readily.

What is a budded rose? A budded rose is a rosebush that is created through a style of grafting known as budding. Two different roses are actually joined together to make one.

Budded roses are easy to identify. They have three parts: The most prominent is the **bud union**. This is the exact spot where the union of the two roses took place. The bud union resembles a swollen knob. It is the separation point between the top part and the root area of the rose. The top part is the desirable rose, the rose you will want to see in your garden. The bottom part is the rootstock. The rootstock is supplying the energy to the bud union. It's from the bud union that the strongest and best growth will emerge season after season.

Over the years, various rootstocks have been used in the budding process. The most successful of these include the species roses *Rosa multiflora* (species roses are given Latin names and sometimes common names) and *Rosa canina* (also known as the 'Dog Rose'); 'Manetti' (an old Noisette); an old red climber 'Dr. Huey'; and for gardens in Florida, an old climber called 'Fortuniana'.

I've singled out Florida is for an important reason. The popular rootstocks 'Dr. Huey', *R. canina*, 'Manetti', and *R. multiflora* cannot survive the onslaught of soil nematodes (microscopic worms that feed on the plant roots; see **September**), which are overabundant in the sandy soil throughout this state. The only rootstock that will survive this is 'Fortuniana'. If you are in Florida and want to grow a budded rose successfully, make sure it is budded on 'Fortuniana'.

**Budded roses are graded, or rated, on a scale of one to three.** This system is based on how many strong canes the plant has. The best quality plants to purchase are roses graded #1, signifying that the plant has *at least* three strong canes. A rating of #2 would indicate two canes, while #3 means one cane or, worse, just a few short stumps coming off the bud union.

Nurseries selling budded roses should state in their catalog the grade of roses they are selling. Of course you should demand #1 at all times. Although #2 and #3 are worth growing and less expensive, you'll need to give them more TLC to bring them up to par with a #1.

You might wonder if there is an advantage to growing budded roses. Yes, there is. A healthy budded rose is a substantial plant capable of producing a strong growing rosebush. Mail-order plants arrive to your home dormant, yet full of vigor, ready to grow. In less than two months

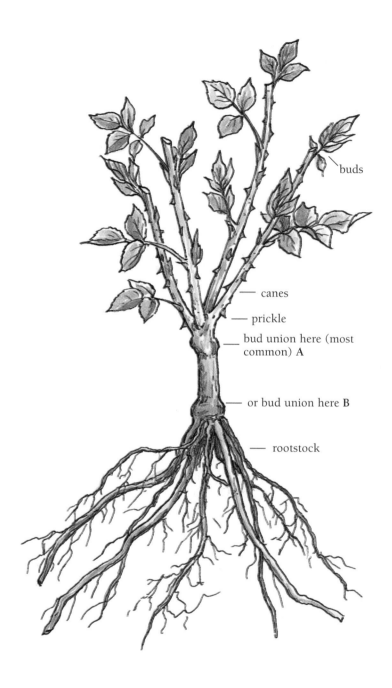

buds

canes

prickle

bud union here (most common) **A**

or bud union here **B**

rootstock

*A and B in this illustration indicate the two possible areas for a bud union. A is more common. The bud union is identified by a swollen knob, easy to spot.*

after planting, a budded rose will start producing beautiful flowers in your garden.

Many experienced rosarians believe there is a worthwhile difference between rootstocks. **The arguments stem from the use of 'Dr. Huey', the most popular of rootstocks in our country.** For instance, many rosarians claim that roses budded onto *Rosa multiflora* are less susceptible to diseases than those budded onto 'Dr. Huey'. There are even claims that the flower quality can be affected by the rootstock, too.

I grow roses on *all* of the available rootstocks, except 'Fortuniana' (this rose will not survive my freezing winters), and 'Manetti' which can be unreliable for winter hardiness as well. What I am careful to note is how the quality of the bud union affects the quality of growth and bloom. Poor budding practices back at the nursery where the rose was originally propagated can lead to poor growth. This nursery has a responsibility to deliver to you a top quality plant of the best grade possible. When you buy the plant, the bud union should be at least two years old and with a substantial amount of swelling.

In the first edition of this book, I wrote: "I'm not sure if I could commit myself with certainty to one position or the other." Well, with an additional nine years of rose growing experience behind me, **I can definitely say that for the northeast and in many other colder areas of the United States, *R. multiflora* has proven to be the best rootstock for budded roses.**

Despite the arguments over which rootstock is best, budded roses make up the largest volume of rosebushes sold today, and most of them are budded onto 'Dr. Huey'.

There are other disadvantages to budded roses besides the possibility of a poor graft creating problems (and there's nothing you can do to make this better). A budded rose can grow poorly, and even die, if your climate is too hot or too cold. How do you know if this applies to you? Consult your local rose society. They've been growing roses for a very long time and they can advise you.

Don't always rely on the nursery for this bit of advice. It's unfortunate but true that some nurseries will sell you budded roses even when they know that the climate where you garden is not right for them. I experienced this once while consulting on a garden in Houston, Texas. One mail-order nursery went so far as to reassure my client that 100 shrub roses he planned on ordering (all budded) would even grow under the shade of a live oak tree. Yeah, right! Fortunately, I headed this one off at the pass. Heed my advice!

If you garden in one of those areas where weather is known for being extreme, and the rose you really want is only available as a budded plant, the try this:

Go ahead and order the rose. Plant it and take cuttings (see **June**) during the season. What you'll be doing is starting new plants of the same variety on their own roots. Eventually, if and when the budded rose dies, you'll have a backup of own-root roses. But, please, don't even *think* of selling your rooted cuttings without checking to see if the rose is protected by a patent.

Another disadvantage to budded roses is the potential of the rootstock growing and taking over. This common occurrence is known as suckering. Suckering could be an indication that the graft is weak, but it could also mean that the rootstock is better suited to your climate than the desirable rose is. (See **June** for more on suckering.)

One very serious problem in dealing with budded roses is the spread of rose viruses. Viruses can only be spread among roses through budding in the nursery. If your plant has a virus, you're stuck with it. Sometimes the growth and flowering potential are affected. Other times it seems to be just a foliage disfigurement that goes away as the season progresses. There are still a great many mysteries about viruses in roses, but one thing is certain: It's the responsibility of the nursery to make sure that all of the plant material is virus free (see **April**).

More and more nurseries today sell roses grown on their own roots. These types of roses are also referred to as **own-root roses**. An own-root rose is simply that—a rose growing on its own root system. Every part, root, top, and all, is desirable. There's no bud union and there's no rootstock.

There are some rose varieties that never seem to adjust to being a budded rose. One such rose that I can think of is the antique beauty 'Gloire de Dijon'. Several times I have tried to grow this **climbing tea** as a budded rose only to have it die during the growing season. The only successful attempt I ever had with this rose was when it was on its own root system. Miniature roses, in my opinion, are difficult to use in the garden as budded roses. I feel that they should only be grown on their own roots. **Budded plants of minis can be too large, defeating the purpose of growing these lovely roses.** I have also noticed a much more natural growth habit from several old garden roses when they are grown on their own root system, but this varies among the different varieties.

When I first started growing roses, own-root roses were treated as a fringe approach to growing roses. At rose meetings, one would hear quiet whispers among a select few who advocated this technique. It seemed to me that the consensus of opinion was that a group of radical rosarians were responsible for this seemingly subversive method of growing roses. Despite this attitude, rooted cuttings were still shared among these rosarians.

*How could one possibly grow a rose without a rootstock? Worse yet, how could you even think of such a thing!* Discussion on the subject of own-root roses was often limited to late-night meetings, **sub rosa,** among the old garden rose fanatics.

This suspicion of roses on their own roots was all very ironic, if not foolish. Before the practice of grafting roses was even conceived, own-root plants were the *only* fashion. It's through this continual sharing of rooted cuttings that we even have roses today. It wasn't until the twentieth century that budded roses became a profitable venture.

Own-root roses have been around for centuries, and they'll be around for many more. Today, nurseries selling roses on their own roots are numerous, and every type of rose and most rose varieties are available to all gardeners as own-root roses. **In recent years there has been a significant increase in the production of own-root roses. They are now included in the inventories of the biggest nurseries that, only a few years ago, were exclusively selling budded roses.**

The most obvious advantage to growing roses on their own roots is that suckering isn't a problem. In fact, it's encouraged. Another advantage was mentioned earlier, but holds enough importance to repeat: Own-root roses will survive temperature extremes better than budded roses. In very cold climates, the top part of an own-root rose can die to the ground over the winter. If the root system is still alive, any new growth sprouting from the roots is desirable. In very hot climates, own-root roses tend to suffer less stress from heat.

Perhaps the biggest advantage of this propagation technique is that **you're less likely to receive a virus-infected plant, provided the nursery you purchased from is propagating from virus-free stock.**

On the practical side, own-root roses can be less expensive than budded roses. But of course there are some disadvantages to own-root roses that you should consider before deserting budded roses entirely.

When you've received your first shipment of own-root roses, your first impulse may be to compost this book. *What is he talking about?* you may wonder. **Be prepared.** These plants will be smaller—considerably smaller—than budded roses. I'm always shocked when I open a long-awaited package to find that my dream climber that supposedly will reach fifteen feet in one season is in reality only 8 inches tall! With the recent resurgence in popularity of own-root roses, many nurseries now send out bigger own-root plants, but they still don't match the starting size of budded roses.

In colder climates it's not unusual for a non-grafted rose to take *at least* two growing seasons to become a respectable size, or at least to reach the size of a newly purchased budded rose of the same variety. But this can differ among individual rose varieties. In the warmest climates, own-root roses will grow fast and will often grow into a nicer shaped plant than a budded rose.

Another disadvantage of own-root roses is that some varieties just don't seem to attain the vigor of the same variety that is budded. This is a hit-and-miss situation, more noticeable when you try to create own-root roses in your garden. The nurseries supplying own-root plants know best which cultivars and varieties are good for own-root, and they also have more expertise to know the best parts of the plants to use for propagating.

Below are the ways roses are propagated. You also need to know the two ways in which a rose can be shipped to your home: Regardless of whether the plant is budded or own-root, a rose can be sent either as a **potted** plant or a **bare-root** plant.

Potted is self-explanatory. The rose arrives on your doorstep ready to grow in a pot. Bare-root means that the rose is not potted. Instead, the roots are naked and vulnerable. Bare-root roses require immediate attention.

**Most mail-order** budded roses are always sent as dormant bare-root plants. Bare-root roses can be a scary sight: tangles of scraggly roots, moist and muddy, with short, plump prickly canes attached. While they're dor-

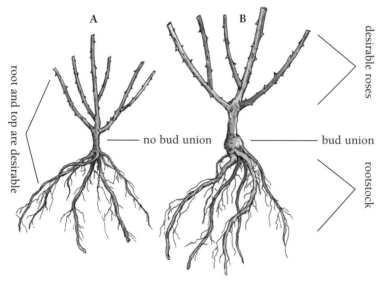

*The most common way to send roses through the mail is without soil around the roots. These are known as bare-root roses. Both own-root (A) and budded roses (B) are shipped bare-root.*

mant, bare-root roses can be shipped all over the country from November through July.

Own-root roses are shipped either as containerized (potted) plants or as bare-root plants. However, it's more likely that an own-root rose will be shipped in a container, including anything from 3-inch plastic sleeves to 8-inch pots. **Potted** is really the best way to get an own-root rose, especially if your garden *might* be frozen when the plant arrives.

Container shipping is costly, and some of the own-root nurseries can't afford this expense. Potted own-root roses will be slightly more expensive than a bare-root version, but worth the extra expense.

I prefer getting own-root roses in pots for one reason: I don't have to rush to get them into the ground. Most own-root roses start their lives as potted roses in the nursery. If they are shipped bare-root, they have to be removed from the pot *before shipping*. The less the roots are disturbed, the better for the plant.

I'm not saying that you shouldn't order from nurseries that ship own-root roses *only* bare-rooted. Those nurseries do exist. But if you are in a cold climate area, you'll have better success with a potted own-root rose.

A potted rose can be shipped at any time of the year, even in full bloom. A bare-root plant (be it budded or own-root) has a limited shipping time. If they order potted, own-root roses, gardeners in cold climates can then receive roses whether they're able to plant them at that time or not. An added plus is that many of the own-root nurseries now offer second-year plants when they ship in pots, meaning the roses are bigger.

In January nearly every mail-order nursery will have begun shipping roses, to warmer climates first. All regions of our country that are frost-free can receive and plant roses in January, whether bare-rooted or in pots. Plants that arrive in January are likely to be dormant. **This is safer, for there is always a danger of those rarely-occurring freezes in warmer regions.**

For colder areas of the country, shipping times will be delayed according to last freeze dates. However, if you really want a rose from a nursery that can only ship bare-root in January or February, and your garden is not going to thaw out until March or later, there is a solution:

This is what you do:
- Store the roses in a cold cellar (above 32 degrees Fahrenheit, but not above 50 degrees Fahrenheit), either under damp peat moss or sphagnum moss
- Or, leave them in the box, store the box in a garage, shed, apple cellar, or anywhere they won't freeze (making sure that they don't become dry)

- Or, have a large hole pre-dug for them outside (perhaps in a vegetable garden) and thickly mulched so that this area won't freeze (mark it so that you know where it is when snow is covering it). Bury them here upon arrival, re-covering them with mulch and adding an additional layer of straw or hay. Leave the roses there until danger of freezing has past (Don't forget to mark the site!).

This might seem like a great deal of information to absorb for one month, but January is the quietest time in everyone's garden. Take advantage of this time to become familiar with the many different nurseries. **Many nurseries have interesting catalogs that make for fun reading.** Some of these are full of important growing tips, beautiful roses, and are more like mini handbooks on rose growing. Others are full of fiction.

Don't forget to go outside and enjoy the solitude of the winter garden, taking notes on changes you could make in the garden or places where you could possibly add more roses, or perhaps, some interesting evergreen shrubs as companions.

## THE FOUR SEASON GARDEN

Your garden should be a four-season garden and adding evergreen shrubs to the design will do just that. This space should be thought of as more than your garden, think of it as an extension of your home. **Like the rooms of your house, the garden should be an inviting and welcome place—every month of the year.** I use all sorts of evergreen shrubs for winter interest and to also create and highlight the design of the garden. Garden designers refer to these elements as the "bones" of the garden.

Boxwoods are among my favorite evergreens for this purpose. 'Graham Blandy' is a columnar boxwood that creates an evergreen vertical element capable of reaching a height of 15 feet and a width of 2 feet; 'Elegantissima', also known as "variegated boxwood", is a shrubby evergreen that can be used to create a low growing variegated hedge or clipped into rounded or square shapes planted as solo specimens in the garden. The more traditional solid green boxwoods—Korean, American, and English, all offer varieties ranging from large shrubby habits to dwarf tidy growths.

If you aren't a fan of boxwoods (some give off an offensive fragrance reminiscent of "cat pee" when they are in bloom), alternatives (and equally elegant as boxwoods) are the many varieties of Japanese hollies, *Ilex crenata*. These hollies have small boxwood-like foliage, often mistaken for boxwoods at a quick glance, and are as versatile. A columnar variety, 'Skypencil', creates a garden exclamation point with its narrow, upright habit. Shrubby varieties such as 'Steed' and 'Soft Touch' make excellent choices for defining a garden space—both good for hedging and sculpting. 'Soft Touch' is a favorite of mine for creating dwarf but wide hedges.

For a different leaf textures, yews (*Taxus*) have both columnar and hedging types available to liven up a winter garden and Arborvitae are available as large tree-like shrubs with a natural pyramidal form.

Warm climate gardeners have an expanded palette of evergreens to choose from. Camellias, with their dark glossy foliage, have the added bonus of rose-like flowers during the winter and the Italian cypress make excellent, tall growing columnar statements.

Look beyond the plants and study the architectural features, or lack of them. You might want to consider adding structures to your garden. You can create off-season beauty by adding an arch to your garden or even a wooden pillar for a rose to climb (see **February**). **A rose garden with structures is no longer just a bed of roses, but an interesting garden with a new dimension.** I discovered that if I lifted and tied the sprawling stems of the old rose 'Mme. Hardy' onto a post, I could create a space in the garden for more roses.

Other thoughts on improving the design or correcting last season's errors go through my head as I enjoy the winter stillness of January. Maybe this year I should tear up that small patch of weedy lawn that was really not worth the trouble to keep up. Or, perhaps this is the year I'll *finally* move those old rosebushes to another part of the garden.

In the colder regions of the country, it might be too cold to actually do any of the physical work involved in making these changes. So, for now, put them down on paper as ideas pop into your head, inspired by your walks through the garden. Later in the season, when the weather cooperates, you can start making the changes.

For everyone, January is a good time to sharpen the cutting blades and oil all the moving parts of your pruning tools; in fact, clean all of your garden tools now. This is a job that I keep putting off until the last moment. I also have to remember to look for my favorite pair of pruning gloves, the ones with the first three fingers cut off for easy tying. But more on them in **February**.

While I'm out walking through the frozen January rose garden, I can't help but think of those lucky gardeners in warmer climates (south Texas, southern California, Florida, and parts of the Southwest), possibly with their roses still in bloom.

A few years ago I attended the annual winter meeting of the Deep South District Rose Society, a group that has members in five southern

*Arches and pillars add interesting architectural features to a winter garden. A series of arches create a rose tunnel.*

states, including Florida. You can imagine my surprise as I was greeted with huge bouquets of fresh-cut roses in the middle of January. The roses ('Dolly Parton') were cut from a garden in Orlando, Florida, that very morning.

Go ahead and boast about your roses while I'm knee deep in snow. But beware: There's always a possibility of a freeze in warmer climates. Even if it might be only for as little as one night, your roses won't be able to defend themselves against this severe weather change. Even a hint of frost could be destructive. As a precaution, I would keep a few spare evergreen boughs of palm fronds handy to throw over your roses and protect the soft new growth.

## PRUNING

If you've migrated to warmer climates, you may have escaped the wrath of northern winters. But you can't escape the responsibility of pruning your roses. January is the time to start pruning if you live where freezes are rare and the sun is warm. Your roses may be in full bloom right now. However, many of your roses could bloom themselves to death if they don't get a period of dormancy, or rest.

Prune all of the plants *and* remove all remaining foliage from your modern roses and cold hardy old garden roses at this time. This creates a dormant rosebush. You'll be rewarded for this "forced" dormancy in a month or so with a new crop of roses. So start pruning and stripping!

Meanwhile, I spend my mornings in the garden plotting a strategy for the pruning that I will hopefully start in February. It's also a good idea to check the winter protection that was put down in December.

By mid-January most nurseries will have started shipping roses to states in the Deep South, the Southwest, and the mild areas of the Northwest. Depending on where you live, you could have a box of roses on your doorstep any day now.

As I wander, I notice rabbit tracks in the snow. Not one or two, but dozens! They seem to be drawn to 'Don Juan', a red climber. Judging from the condition of the snow around the base of this rose and the scraped bark, it seems there was an orgy on this very spot (a tribute to 'Don Juan'?). No doubt there will be many bunnies in time for Easter. Yes, rabbits are cute, but once you see canes of your favorite roses scraped raw, you'll agree: The rabbits are beginning to overstay their welcome.

## RECOMMENDED READING
*Combined Rose List 2006*
   A source list for all roses, compiled and edited by Beverly R. Dobson and Peter Schneider. An annual publication. Cost is $20, from: Peter Schneider, PO Box 677, Mantua, OH 44255
   Website: **www.combinedroselist.com**
   Email: **ComRoseLst@cs.com**

## RECOMMENDED MEMBERSHIP
American Rose Society, PO Box 30,000, Shreveport, LA 71119-0030
   318-938-5402; Email: ars@ars-hq.org
   Website: **www.ars.org**
   Many membership classifications available

## COMPANIONS TO CONSIDER
**Evergreen Shrubs**
   Boxwood 'Graham Blandy', 'Elegantissima', 'Suffruticosa'
   *Ilex crenata* 'Skypencil', 'Steed', 'Soft Touch'
   *Taxus baccata* 'Fastigiata'
   *Cupressus sempervirens* 'Swane's Golden Italian Cypress'
   Arborvitae

# February

It was during my second February as a rosarian that I attended my first rose society meeting. I gave a presentation on the roses of the Cranford Rose Garden, and by the time I was onto my tenth slide, I could sense tension in the room. Perhaps these seasoned rosarians didn't know what to make of this new face in the crowd, or they were just bored. I began to get nervous, losing my confidence quickly as I heard loud voices from the back of the room. "That's not 'Peggy Ann Landon', it's 'American Pillar'," and, "That one's 'Marie Pavié', not 'White Pet'!" Actually, I didn't mind; it was possible I had the names wrong. I knew many of the roses in the garden were mislabeled, and I had used the garden roses as the basis of my lecture. But this was only the beginning.

After an hour of near riot, I thought I had escaped my first experience with the old rose experts relatively unharmed—and entertained them as well —but it wasn't over. I was about to meet the dowager queen of the society. She cornered me and accused me of killing Ophelia. (I was totally unaware that Ophelia was a rose, nor was I in the mood for such an impassioned encounter) What, I wondered, had I gotten myself into? That was it, I had my fill of staying indoors, and when I got back to the garden, I started pruning!

## PRUNING

Pruning in February? Yes. In fact, every rosarian soon learns that pruning is a twelve-month-a-year job. Different times of the year call for different types of pruning, and where you live and garden is a determining factor as to what and when you prune. Warm weather gardeners should be well into pruning by Valentine's Day, while northern gardeners are still wondering if the snow will ever go away. February is as good a time as ever to review the basics of pruning rosebushes. These basics of pruning are for all climates, not just here in my New Jersey garden.

Pruning is simple if you keep a single thought in mind while oiling up your pruners: **Among the worst things you can do for a rose is *not* prune it.**

Pruning revitalizes the plant, encourages new growth each season,and creates an attractive-shaped bush for the garden. Most important, regular pruning helps prevent the spread of diseases and discourages undesirable insects. Consider pruning as "health care" for roses.

It's absolutely essential that the cuts are clean, and to do this you must have the right type of pruners, I use a pruner that cuts like a pair of scissors. Any other type, such as the anvil pruners common among florists, will not cut a rosebush properly. Anvil pruners will damage the plants, often crushing the stems as they cut. A crushed cane will allow more chances for water to get into the wound, beginning the deterioration of the rose cane. Save your anvil type of pruners for making flower arrangements with your cut roses.

When you shop for pruning tools (the handheld pruners are also known as secateurs) you will no doubt find many brands at various price ranges. Unless you're in one of those ridiculously expensive garden boutiques, the prices do reflect the quality of the tools. The rule that's true in most things is also true here: You get what you pay for. When possible, buy a pruner that has a blade designed to be taken apart easily for cleaning, or have its blades replaced when necessary. All of my tools have bright red handles. It's not that this brand is better than any other; it's the color that's important to me—a very practical person. Red-handled tools show up a lot faster when you drop them or lose them in the garden. I'm always losing my garden tools, and the red handles are easy to spot. It's also a good idea to have a holster for the pruners and an apron with a pouch (those carpenter aprons with all the nail pockets are really cool, and are perfect for this job).

To begin, take a cane (the rose stem) in your gloved hand. First notice its texture and color. Not all roses have green canes—some have purple, red, or even a combination of colors. Cane color should be fairly consistent within a plant. Those canes with unusual discoloration or severe looking blotches should be removed (see **March** regarding canker). If the cane has a shriveled, prune-like appearance instead of a smooth finish, or if the wood snaps easily when bent, the cane is dead. Besides being unattractive, dead wood is an open door to insects and disease. Remove it.

Next, take out weak, spindly canes and any crossing branches from the center of the plant. (This should become second nature to you when you start pruning.) These create clutter, hindering the circulation of air through the bush, and provide a perfect breeding place for unwelcome pests or diseases.

After all of this, the remaining canes should be shortened. But before pruning frenzy sets in, one rule does apply: Each cut should be made above a bud eye (growing point). Bud eyes are located along the length of every cane. They are in a spiral arrangement as you go down the cane. Bud eyes should show a slight swelling or even a distinct red color at pruning time. They eventually develop into new branches that will terminate with a flower. The farther down the cane (away from the tip) the bud eye is located, the stronger and larger the new bloom will be.

Select a plump bud eye and make the cut about one-fourth of an inch above. Cut at an angle with the bud toward the top of the slant. Bud eyes point in the direction that new growth will occur, and those closest to the cut will become the main growing points, so it's important to prune to a bud pointing *away* from the center of the shrub.

How far you shorten a cane, choosing which cane you shorten, and which cane you leave longer, depends greatly on the type of rose and how the rose is going to be used in the garden. These decisions all fall under the task of shaping a rose shrub. The shape the rose bush takes on in your garden is initially determined by your pruning. Different types of roses require different types of shaping, all determined by the growth habit of that rose. This will be covered as I introduce the different types of garden roses.

These are the general pruning rules for all roses, no matter where you garden, and whether you're in Seattle or Miami. It's *when* to prune that differs among the different climates of our country, and different types of roses should get pruned at different times of the year. The time to start your early season pruning is pretty much dictated by the weather.

Freezing weather signals the end of the rose-growing season for many gardeners. A cold period holds the roses in a dormant phase, during which energy is stored in the canes, bud union, and roots until the signal for growth happens. Warm days and pruning are the signals to start serious growth.

If you garden in a warm climate, then pruning signals both the end and the beginning. Roses in warm climates are more likely to suffer damage from a cold snap than the same roses growing in a cold region. When those inevitable cold fronts push through, often the new rose growth is too young to survive a sudden drop to freezing temperatures. For this reason, warm weather gardeners should be careful not too prune if there is still a chance of a freeze occurring in their area. Even the toughest roses can suffer some damage from a dip into freezing temperatures. It's best to wait to start pruning after the temperatures are back to normal.

Before I introduce the rose classes I prune in February, look over the following questions in regard to blooming and growth habits of roses. This will help you further enjoy your roses. As a supplement to this section, I have created an appendix for this edition listing the main rose types with their growth habits and pruning notes for each class.

There are many rose classes, and not all of them have the same blooming characteristics, the biggest differences being when they bloom and how often they bloom.

### • Is the rose an ever-bloomer or a once-bloomer?

Roses that bloom all season flower on *all* growth produced during the *current* season *and* from previous year's growth. These are referred to as **repeating roses, or ever-bloomers.** They benefit from a severe annual pruning that could mean removing as much as two-thirds of the existing plant.

Roses that only bloom once during the season are often referred to as non-repeating roses, **or once-bloomers.** They need to have at least a year's worth of growth to produce a respectable amount of bloom the following season since they produce their best roses from the older growth (last year's canes). Leave a great deal of old wood intact when pruning these— as much as your garden space will allow.

There are thousands of different roses, each of them belonging to a rose class or type. The different classes fall under two headings: **old garden roses** and **modern roses.**

Some examples of the old garden rose classes are gallicas, damasks, tea, and China roses. Examples of modern rose classes are polyanthas, hybrid teas, climbers, and English roses. Within both categories of old and modern, there are both repeat-blooming roses and non-repeat bloomers.

### • Does the rose produce hips?

Rose hips are the berry-like or apple-shaped remains of the flower. They start to develop as soon as the rose is pollinated. By the time the petals have fallen, the rose hip should be obvious. Rose hips are not fruits, but instead are receptacles for fruit and seeds of the rose. Nearly every rose is capable of producing a hip.

Rose hips are an extra colorful feature to consider in your garden, especially noticeable in the winter. They range in color from dark purple to vermillion to bright cherry red. Some are smooth and shiny, others are dull and bristly. The sizes and shapes of rose hips are various, too, from egg shapes to those reminiscent of a pendant or a fluted flask.

Rose hips signal the completion of the cycle of a rose bush. As with other flowering plants, the rosebush has a goal to produce a seed for future generations. As a rose hip develops, and the seeds become more mature, the flower production on repeat-blooming roses slows down. To prevent this, the faded flower is removed, or deadheaded (see **June**), before the rose hip develops. This encourages further blooming. This is not a concern with once-blooming roses, because they've already accomplished their goal. Find out whether or not your rose will bloom again this season (ask an expert, or wait and see). If it's not going to re-bloom till next year, then you can leave the faded blooms intact and watch the hips develop.

- **Is the rose a climber or a shrub?**

Knowing the growth habit of your rose is important when making pruning decisions. Roses meant to climb shouldn't get pruned as severely as a plant that's meant to be a short shrub.

Get to know your rose. Watch how it grows. Maybe wait a season before pruning, or prune sparingly until you are better acquainted. It won't take long for the rose you bought, or inherited with a new/old house, to give you a clue to its preferred growing habit and blooming cycle. Patience will pay off.

Some roses are very responsive to pruning: Their buds start growing almost immediately after their canes have been shortened. This is true among the ever-blooming roses of the China and tea classes, as well as their immediate blood relatives, Noisettes and Bourbon roses. But caution should be taken as to when you prune them: Make sure that the danger of frost is behind you.

Other rose classes that are ever-blooming, but a bit further removed from their China and tea relatives, can tolerate some degree of cold even just after they've been pruned. These rose classes include hybrid teas, floribundas, grandifloras, shrub roses, miniatures, polyanthas, hybrid perpetuals, Portland roses, and many climbers.

What do I prune in February? I select roses that have the slowest response to being cut; the ones that remain dormant until the growing conditions are right. If by chance there is a freeze after they start growing, they'll suffer minimal damage.

To start my pruning in February gives me an opportunity to focus more attention on the shaping and training of these roses. On the practical side, this also lightens my spring chores.

Within the old garden roses group, I go after species roses and European old garden roses (the cold-hardy, once-bloomers). Within the modern roses, I can be found tearing my clothes and shedding blood as I wrestle with shrub roses and climbers. Below is a brief look into these classes and some specific pruning tips for each.

# MODERN ROSES

Within the large group known as Modern roses I prune shrub roses and climbers in February. It's difficult to determine where the boundary between shrub roses and climbers falls: Technically speaking, both are shrubs. As these classes first evolved, shrub roses were those that maintained a graceful shrub habit while the climbers were roses capable of being trained onto structures. As the shrub class became more popular, many newer introductions didn't seem to know their limits on growth style, or which class they really belonged to.

I witnessed this blending of personalities while visiting a rose trial field in Lyons, France. One of the leading French nurseries breeding new shrub roses is under the supervision of Alain Meilland. It's in Alain's blood to know a good rose when he sees one (it was Alain's father who gave us the 1944 rose 'Peace', one of the most popular and successful roses ever introduced).

All of the roses in his fields are tested in every possible growing situation. One rose cultivar, for example, is grown in three different fashions: trained as a climber, clipped regularly as a shrub, and grown without any pruning or care whatsoever. Whichever habit suits the rose best will determine the way this new rose is marketed, ultimately being classed as a climbing rose or a shrub rose.

## SHRUB ROSES

It might seem redundant to have a class titled shrub roses when actually *all* roses are shrubs. One sometimes suspects that whoever decided on this title couldn't think of a genuinely new category and decided to throw all of the oddball types together.

That's not entirely true. There is one characteristic that draws this enormous class together. A true shrub rose should look good in the garden on its own with an attractive growth habit. The shape of the plant should have a natural grace to it. For example, the new shrub rose 'Carefree Delight' (a Meilland introduction) has a gorgeous arching habit, displaying blooms from *all parts* of the plant, not just from the top. This is what a shrub rose should do. But, before we go on, I have one criticism of this rose and any other rose marketed as "carefree." They never actually are.

Rustling canes and frightened rabbits give away the whereabouts of my rose garden volunteers during cold February mornings. They'll disappear, for what seems like hours, under the mounded, green prickly canes of 'Carefree Delight' and 'Carefree Wonder' planted on the hillside. I know that when Bob and Sue finally reappear, with shredded clothing and muddy knees, they'll have gathered a bounty of deadwood. If nothing else,

*Shrub roses usually have attractive growth habits. Some can be upright with lax canes (A) while others exhibit lower, ground-hugging growth habits (B)*

there's always deadwood to remove. All roses will always provide this, including the "carefree" shrub varieties.

The class shrub rose can be divided into two subgroups: ever-blooming and once-blooming shrub roses. Unless the plant has a winter hip display, I prune once-blooming shrubs now as well.

## CLIMBERS

Climbing roses are tall growing and wide-spreading shrub roses that produce clusters of large flowers on long, long canes. In some literature you may see these referred to as "large-flowered climbers." They are not truly climbing plants in that they don't produce vines, nor do they have the natural ability to climb completely on their own. Ivy can climb: It uses tendrils for attaching to a wall. Wisteria can climb: The fast growing stems wrap themselves around any available structure. Roses can't perform either of these feats. To cover a fence, a wall, or a house, a climbing rose needs assistance. You must tie it to whatever structure the plant is meant to cover.

Sometimes a very long cane can become lodged in the crotch of a tree or become snagged onto the gutter of a house. In these instances the prickles serve as anchors, holding the canes in place as they continue to grow. But otherwise, unless the canes are secured, it is likely that they will whip around in the wind or collapse to create a large mound, and smother everything planted nearby in the garden.

Generally referred to as "climbers", these roses grow in various manners. Some produce long canes from the base of the plant, while others attain their widespread growth and height from growth that emerges from various points along older wood.

As with the shrub rose class, this group can be further divided into two subgroups: once-bloomers and ever-bloomers. In the winter, I prune the ever-bloomers and all once-bloomers that were left untouched during the season because of their beautiful hip display ('American Pillar', 'Silver Moon', 'City of York' are examples).

There is significant variety within the class of climbers. Candidates for this category should not be limited strictly to roses included in the American Rose Society's approved class of climbing roses. There are many members of other classes that deserve to be used as climbers, especially among some of the warm weather ever-blooming roses such as Noisettes, Bourbons, hybrid Chinas, hybrid Noisettes, hybrid Bourbons, hybrid musk, climbing teas, and climbing Chinas. These are all rose classes with varieties suitable for covering arbors and pergolas in warmer climates.

It's important to consider all roses as individual, each reacting differently to the climate you garden in. The climbing habit can either be exaggerated or kept in check by climate. Some climbers are limited to short shrubs because of cold winters. In the warmest climates, on the contrary, almost any rose can be grown as a climber.

Another group of climbers that will be discussed later are ramblers. These are once blooming climbers that produce very pliable canes and massive displays of small flowers in clusters. The significant pruning of this group happens in mid season (see **July**).

The winter following the second season of bloom is prime time to launch your first pruning assault on shrubs and climbers, since it usually takes at least two seasons for these plants to reach their full potential. Both classes are pruned in similar fashions, the chief difference being that, if you have a climber, you want to make sure you leave the long canes long. Hopefully you are going to train these onto a structure (more on that later).

The tools for this job are a pair of secateurs, a lopper (a long-handled pruner), a small pruning saw, protective clothing, and a sturdy pair of leather gloves. Try to find a pair with an extended cuff to protect your forearm. I always tell my volunteers you need to leave some blood behind in order to get the job done right. You can't help but do that with these vigorous roses.

Examine the plant thoroughly from every possible angle. Can you see through the plant, or, are there crowded spots caused by crossing canes or dense piles of deadwood?

Here's how I prune shrub roses and climbers in February:

- **First step**: remove the deadwood

I find that removing deadwood is a great warm-up exercise, especially on those cold February mornings. It also puts you in the right frame of mind for the next step.

- **The second step**: remove live wood

I call this thinning out the plant. The purpose of thinning is to open the plant, giving the remaining canes freedom of movement and room to grow. The goal is to create as beautiful a shape as possible, but you're also allowing the plant to channel its energy to the strongest wood.

Start by eliminating all crossing, rubbing, and entangled canes, simply cutting below where the canes cross each other. You can stop here. You've eliminated all of the deadwood and the clutter and you still have a plant to enjoy. But maybe the plant is not looking too balanced, possibly because there are still too many canes.

- **The third step**: remove *more* wood.

Go ahead and cut some more, but pay attention to what you're doing. You should be aware of where every branch is going. Take your time and follow each cane from its origin to the finish (Don't forget to breathe!). Locate where the newer growth originates. This may be from the base of the plant or from random points along an old cane. Your goal here is to take out old wood. But before you cut, make sure that the treasured new wood you are keeping is not growing from the old wood you are removing (oops!).

Older wood should be easy to spot. It's tough looking, with thicker bark that is sometimes a gray or brown color, and maybe even peeling. Some of the old wood might also carry the remains of the last season's flowers—perhaps hips or twigs from the clusters.

When deciding how many canes to remove and how many to leave behind, a general rule is to prune away up to one-third of the plant. I know this might seem drastic, but the old wood you remove will be quickly replaced during the season by healthy, vigorous new growth. So, make room for it now.

If you've made it this far and you still have a bush in front of you, here's your next step.

- **The fourth step**: shorten side shoots.

Hold a cane and look at it from tip to base. If there are any side shoots coming off this cane, shorten them to anywhere from 3 to 6 inches long. Do this to each of the remaining canes. This is especially important with a climbing rose. These side shoots (or laterals) will produce the biggest flower clusters in the next season.

- **The fifth step**: cut the tips.

The last step is really easy. You've made it through the tough part, now it's just a matter of cutting the tip of every cane to encourage the development of more side shoots during the next growing season. You can be creative and make the canes slightly different lengths. This will make a more interesting shape as the plant begins to grow. For a climber, or for a shrub that you want to train as a climber, leave enough long canes for covering your structure.

The final outcome of your pruning exercise—how tall, short, or wide the final pruned plant should be—depends greatly on *your* garden, and how *you* intend to use the plant. Also, the mood you were in when you started might have something to do with the huge pile of compost you've just created! Are your still afraid to prune? Wait until you are having a bad day. Then go to the garden and take out your frustrations on your roses! I always feel better after a long pruning session with 'Dr. W. Van Fleet'.

These pruning tips apply to the old garden roses group, too, with a few modifications. Here's some background information on these roses, followed by pruning instructions.

# OLD GARDEN ROSES

## SPECIES ROSES

These are the original roses, wild roses predating all of us. They've been around for a very, very long time, since long before humans invented the word "pruning".

Species are usually identified in catalogs and books with a Latin name, such as *Rosa rugosa*. There are many species hybrids that also belong to this group, including **rugosa hybrids, eglantine hybrids, foetida hybrids, and spinosissima hybrids**.

Since most of the species roses are prolific hip producers, if you have to prune them you should wait until the hips have lost their beauty.

It's easy to prune a species rose. Remove deadwood annually and then thin out the oldest wood only when the natural beauty of the plant shape is lost due to excess clutter. Otherwise, prune these roses when they become invasive to the rest of your garden. You can either shovel-prune them, or do what I do when my *Rosa davurica* oversteps its boundaries: I prune it with a lawn mower.

Here's the first insect pest of the year: Though not a very common problem, **rose stem girdler** is a frequent visitor among many of the species roses and their hybrids. At this time of year it is easy to spot the swelling along the canes caused by the overwintering larvae of this very small beetle. As the weather warms up the grubs will become active, feeding on the sap of the rose as it begins to rise, and eventually causing dieback of the cane.

It's easy to control this infrequent guest. Look for swellings on canes and remove those canes, making a cut below the swelling.

## EUROPEAN OLD GARDEN ROSES
Included in this group are cold-hardy, once-blooming roses that provided the petals for the ancient Romans to frolic in; the roses the Pilgrims carried across the sea; and those that modern-day historians argue over incessantly. The following classes are represented in this group: gallica, alba, damask, centifolia, and moss roses.

I do most of my pruning of these in midsummer (see **July**). They bloom best when they are encouraged to have strong summer growth— this is the growth that will produce the next season's roses. In February, they should only be lightly pruned and cleaned up.

I do the following: Remove deadwood, damaged canes, anything that is out-of-bounds, and shorten any side shoots coming off of long canes, in the same manner as the ever-blooming shrubs and climbers.

Finish the job by shortening the remaining canes, either by just cutting tips or shortening them 1 or 2 inches.

If you have an old plant that hasn't been pruned, or one that was displaying hips ('Alain Blanchard', 'Old Red Moss', 'Trigintipetala', 'Complicata'), then follow the same rules for pruning shrub roses and climbers. But do more thinning than shortening of canes.

You can skip a year of pruning with these roses: Be guided by the way you have them on display in the garden. They always look best when grown in as natural a shape as possible.

Who said old garden roses are immune to problems? **Rose scale** is an armored sucking insect that enjoys the sap of roses, especially these roses.

It's easier to spot scale when the infestation is severe. Resembling speckled white powder on the lowest areas of the canes, this insect will build up clusters of powdery mounds on the lower canes of the roses. I see it most often among large shrubs of old roses (especially moss roses) and species roses. Neglected climbers, hybrid teas, and floribundas that are left untouched for many years, full of deadwood and clutter, will often have scale.

In my experience, roses growing in shade seem more likely to have scale infestation than roses growing in full sun. To control this pest, remove as much of the infested wood as possible. **Dormant oil** (a horticultural oil meant to be sprayed while a plant is without foliage) *or* **Lime-sulfur** (a sulfur-based pesticide—*do not mix this with any oil sprays!*) sprayed now—perhaps two applications—should do the trick. Just spraying once has kept this pest under control in my gardens. Do not use any of these dormant sprays when the temperature is warmer than 75 degrees Fahrenheit or else you may burn the foliage of the roses. The oil or lime-sulfur will also kill over-wintered fungal spores that can cause black spot, mildew and rust, as well as the eggs of spider mites and aphids. You can't get a better bargain than this.

This is where *my* February pruning ends. For gardeners in Texas, warm and temperate climates of the west coast, along the Gulf Coast, and right up into coastal Carolinas, Valentine's Day signals the time to start pruning *all* your roses. I'll discuss the other rose classes, as I get to them in *my* garden. Despite the cold winters, I manage to grow varieties from ever rose class.

Up here in the colder climates, I take it slow. I don't rush spring. These roses I just pruned can tolerate a cold temperature after pruning. Hybrid teas and others might show some damage from severe cold if you prune too early. I wait until March before I attack any other roses.

If you can tolerate the cold weather and you've pruned the roses from the list above, now you might want to train them onto a structure, if that's your intention.

My parents had a rose growing on a split rail fence in front of our home in New Jersey. I remember huge sprays of pink spilling everywhere in June and throughout the summer. By autumn, there were long whipping branches that would grab anybody passing by. In fact, I suspect that this unruly behavior was what led to its eviction from our front yard. It had outgrown the fence. But, until the day it was removed, the pruning required hedge shears and armor to keep it in bounds.

The long canes that hung so menacingly over the heads of my friends on their way to school was a clue that this rose must have been a climbing rose. I wonder: If it had been trained properly onto a higher fence or lattice, maybe it would not have been considered such a threat to the neighborhood and would still be there today!

There are several possibilities for structures that can be used to train and contain vigorous roses such as the pink monster of my childhood, and there is a right way to train a climber or a vigorous shrub rose onto a structure in order to get it to bloom to its maximum capability.

In addition to the basic pruning equipment, you will need a ladder, soft twine (I prefer jute) and, most of all, patience. I have special gloves for this job. When I have to train and tie, I wear a pair of leather gloves with the thumb and first two fingers cut halfway off. This homemade design enables me to tie and still have some protection from the prickles of the roses.

A wall can offer countless opportunities for the training of a rosebush. But as beautiful as a wall of roses might appear, it can also be a great deal of trouble to create. I personally never look forward to attaching a rose directly to a wall. I've done it when asked, but it's a difficult job. I much prefer an attached structure, such as a lattice, for training roses onto walls. However, there are times when the architecture of the house or landscape requires that you attach the roses directly to the wall.

I've had great success attaching roses to stucco walls using machine screws, lead anchors, and cable wire clips –all inexpensive materials available from your local hardware store. As the canes of the rosebush become long enough to train, I mark the spot on the wall with a pencil where I want to secure the branch. At this mark, drill a hole with a $1/4$-inch mason drill bit, about $1/2$ inch to $3/4$ inch into the wall (the depth of this hole depends on the size of the anchor you are using). I insert the lead anchor into the hole and screw in the clip (I prefer lead instead of the colored plastic anchors- the gray color of the lead anchor is easier to hide). The clip is a small plastic (clear or white) loop that is used by telephone and cable companies to secure their cables to your house. You simply tie the rose cane to this clip. The result of this work is that the rose appears to be secured without any visible attachment—a nice effect! As the rose continues to grow, you'll need to add more clips, that is, until you run out of wall space. At that point, simply prune the long rose canes to keep them within the designated space.

Solid stone and brick walls are not as easy to work with. In order to secure the rose to this type of wall, you need to hammer mortar nails into the cement between the bricks or stone. The rose is then tied at each nail. It's not an easy task to permanently lodge the nails into the mortar of the wall. I know I'm guaranteed to get sore thumbs since I'm not very good with a hammer. You could also try drilling into the brick or stone using a mortar drill bit and securing the rose with lead anchors and cable clips.

There is an alternative to all this hammering and drilling: small hooks that you attach to the wall with an adhesive. I've discovered that these are not as permanent as the manufacturer promises. Severe changes in temperature and humidity eventually cause the hooks to come off of the wall. In addition to problems from weather, often the weight of the rose canes will pull them off the wall as well.

It's much easier to train roses onto a wall if you have some sort of structure, such as a lattice either attached directly to the wall or supported by posts up close to the wall. Either of these styles or perhaps a lattice by itself, in the middle of the garden as a freestanding wall or fence, serves as a wonderful way to show off a vigorous-spreading rose.

The **lattice** is a classic structure for a rose, with many designs to choose from or create. A lattice can be as big as you need and as elaborate or as simple in design as you please. One thing a lattice offers that a solid wall doesn't is free air movement through the structure and around the plant. And depending on the design of the lattice, there can be as many places as necessary for tying rose canes.

When I work with a lattice, I imagine it to be a ladder for the climber. I've designed lattice panels with one-inch horizontal lathes spaced a foot apart; other designs have rectangular patterns; and often I've used square openings. The one-inch wide horizontal lathes serve as the "rungs" for the rose canes to attach to.

As the rose matures, I make sure each winter to tie one cane to each lathe. Eventually every lathe will have a cane.

By the way, use only a soft material for tying; never use plastic or wire (especially not plastic bag ties). I use jute, a natural twine. Old nylons, cut into strips, are also very good. I've seen many beautiful climbers die back because the canes were cut, or girdled, by wires or plastic used to attach them to the lattice.

You'll get the best flowers from your rose if you spread it out on the lattice as much as you possibly can. One easy way is to train it into a fan shape.

On your lattice or wall, create an imaginary center line, perpendicular to the ground and running right through the center of the plant. This is the center line of the fan design. Whatever you train to one side of the fan, try to mirror it on the other side. The goal is to have equal amounts of canes on both sides of this mark, curving outward and downward, away from the center of the plant.

Separate the longest canes into two groups. Half of the canes are for one side, the remainder for the other. Before you tie anything, just mentally arrange the canes so that one will go up to the top of the lattice,

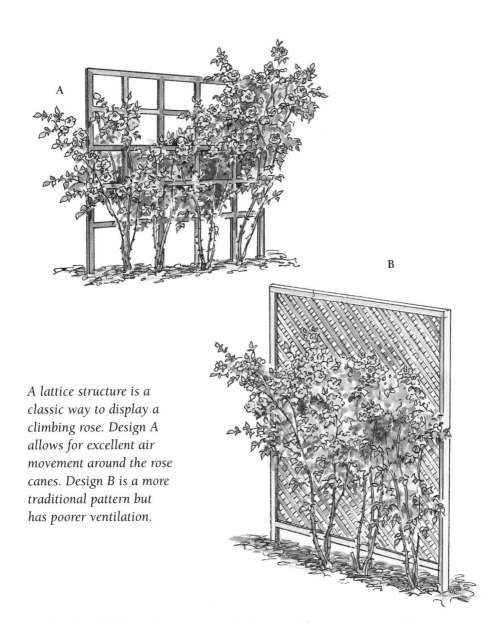

A

B

*A lattice structure is a classic way to display a climbing rose. Design A allows for excellent air movement around the rose canes. Design B is a more traditional pattern but has poorer ventilation.*

one in the middle, and one nearer the bottom. If you can set up six canes, three on each side of the imaginary line, you'll be off to a good start. Then if you have more canes, you can add them into the design, spacing them as close as 6 inches or 1 foot apart. If you have only one or two canes to work with, stretch them as far as they will go. Your goal is to get as much coverage as possible without crowding the design.

Take your longest cane and tie it to the lattice. As you train it, make sure that at some point the cane becomes horizontal, if only briefly, and ends with a downward curve. Do this with each cane. Remember that what you do on one side of the design you repeat on the other.

The graceful curves create a beautiful design for the winter garden. But that's not the only reason the canes are trained in this manner. Every time a cane is trained horizontally, this encourages more side branches to grow off of that particular cane. Each side shoot will produce blooms. If the canes were trained straight up the lattice, most of the blooms would end up near the top of the lattice.

Tie the canes to the structure, in as many places as it takes to keep the canes secure. As you finish tying each cane, prune a few inches off the tip. This further encourages the development of side shoots.

Each winter you will have more and more canes to use. The goal is to cover the lattice with as much of the rosebush as possible. Eventually, you will have more canes than you need. When this happens, remove one-third of the plant (oldest wood first) to make room for newer canes. Never remove from the lattice a cane that you can't replace with a newer one.

If you have some room in front of the lattice, you can let a few canes hang free of the structure and into the bed. This will add to the lushness of the display. Prune these canes to various lengths, some short some longer, to give a natural look yet keeping them from overtaking the garden or space in front of the lattice.

In addition to covering walls, lattice panels can be used in many ways to improve the design of your garden. A single lattice, or a series of lattice, can create a fence or boundary for the garden or used to create privacy. If both sides of the lattice are in your garden, plant roses on both sides. Two panels at right angles to each other create a corner in the garden. Lattice can also be used as a windscreen on an exposed site. In this situation, and for creating privacy, I would use a tighter lattice pattern, such as the typical diamond style, with one-inch openings. I've used 'New Dawn' (a vigorous climbing rose) in Manhattan penthouse gardens to give my clients privacy and to spare them the views of ugly buildings across the way. In these high wind exposure sites, the rose, of course, should then be planted on the leeward side.

The reward for all of this work will be a wall of roses. Any climbing rose or sprawling shrub rose, old or modern, can be trained in this manner.

There are many variations on freestanding structures that can be placed smack in the middle of a flower bed or a lawn, be attached to a planting box, or introduced just about anywhere there is sun. A **tripod** is the very basic form and the easiest to construct. It's simply three pillars arranged to lean on each other coming together at a point. A height of ten feet for the peak of the tripod is best, since this will show off your roses dramatically.

A **pyramid** of roses can be constructed in the same manner by adding one more pillar. If you want to be more creative, you can close the sides of the pyramid with panels of lattice, or even wrought iron. An elegant finishing touch, reminiscent of nineteenth-century French rose gardens, could be a finial such as a sphere or an urn. I suppose you could call this an **obelisk**, adding a touch of class to your garden.

The goal here is twofold: to show off the roses to their best advantage, and to give your garden something of interest when the roses aren't in bloom. Let your instincts and pocketbook guide you on structure design.

It's best to plant the pillars at the same time you plant the rose. Otherwise you have the risk of damaging the root system of the rose as well as becoming seriously wounded and spilling blood when you become entangled with these vigorous plants as you attempt to add a pillar or two. But, nothing is ever perfect in the garden world. Quite often the structure is an afterthought or a necessity as the rose soon out grows its allotted space. So, with a posthole digger, try to be as careful as possible. But remember, spilt blood around roses is good fertilizer!

It can be especially beautiful to combine ever-blooming shrub roses with old garden roses to cover your structures. Plant one rose at each corner and wrap the canes around the individual posts if your structure is open, or wrap from corner to corner. You can crisscross canes or run them all in one direction, parallel to each other. Every time you wrap the canes around the structure, you break the vertical climb of the rose and induce the dormant bud eyes to grow. The result will be a lush display of blooms covering the entire structure.

Consider adding vines to the structures as companions for your climbing roses. Annual vines, such as morning glories and the fragrant moonflower vine add cool colors and fragrance. A classic perennial mate would be clematis. All clematis would work fine with roses, you can choose from early season bloomers, continual bloomers, and autumn blooming cultivars. Climbing hydrangea and wisteria are two other plants that blend well with roses. Both of these woody vines provide thick stems that are good places to attach rose canes. One of the more unusual, but interesting, vines to use with roses is the climbing lily, *Gloriosa superba* 'Rothschildiana'. This tender vine is a perennial in Central Florida and rosarians down there often use this for color on their arches during the summer heat period when the roses are in semi-dormant, non-blooming phase.

You don't have to grow a vigorous rose onto a structure. **Try letting them grow free of any support.** If properly pruned, shrub roses (modern and old) often look best when planted in groups of three. Spacing them three feet from each other, one variety per group, will create mounds of color.

*Climbing roses are very tall-growing and/or wide-spreading shrub roses. They need to be tied to a support to achieve a "climbing" habit. Tripods and pyramidal structures are interesting devices for displaying climbers and shrubs.*

Climbing roses might be too aggressive for a small garden if left to grow free. But if you have the space, one climber on its own, properly pruned, can be a gorgeous site. An alternative plan could be to use them as a hedge planting, spacing them 4 to 6 feet apart. If you stagger the planting, you can get more plants into less space and have a wider hedge.

At the Mendocino Coast Botanical Gardens in Fort Bragg, California, gardeners have successfully created a deer deterrent with plantings of shrub roses and climbing roses. The shrub roses are planted in clumps. The climbers are trained onto staggered eight foot by four-foot sections of fencing. Apparently this confuses the deer, keeping them out of the garden.

City living has given me a new viewpoint on gardening with roses. There are definitely some advantages to using tall growing roses in sites that you many not have considered. I planted several fast-growing climbing roses ('New Dawn', 'Altissimo', 'Sombreuil', and 'Compassion') with the sole intent of improving the security system for a client in Brooklyn. Why use razor wire when you can have two feet of arching, prickly canes over the top of a wall and something the razor wire won't give you—a beautiful floral display!

# MARCH

Walking down the street during March, I can spot deadwood at fifty paces and I can never resist the temptation. My trusty pruners are hanging from my belt and I'm prepared to pull them out with the speed of a gunfighter to make the cut.

By March, pruning has become an obsession. I close my eyes at night and see stubby canes. While visiting friends' gardens, I want to start crawling around under their rose plants and remove diseased wood (that's tough to do without insulting them!). At the same time, it is more than coincidence to suddenly be at the top of the invitation list for afternoon luncheons when the host has a garden full of unpruned roses. Most of my friends know that pruners are a permanent attachment to my body in March, and my number one pastime for the moment is pruning, as it is for most rosarians across the country.

From the crack of dawn to late at night (yes, even with flashlights), rose pruning fever is sweeping the nation during March. This is the month of the year when most rosarians across the country are taking a rabbit's-eye view of their roses.

When I first started growing roses, I would leave all of my pruning for March, hesitating every time a frost blew through, or worse, a late winter snowfall—all the time waiting patiently for the forsythia to bloom. "**Prune when the forsythia bloom**" was the golden rule passed down from one generation of rosarians to the next, serving as a safe guide for all who are unsure of when to begin chopping.

I began to experiment and discovered that I could bend this rule a little by starting to prune in February (see **February**). By doing this, I could get the garden finished by the time the forsythia reached its peak bloom in April.

In March, the sun starts getting noticeably stronger and the days longer. Spring is around the corner; the roses are showing signs of breaking dormancy. Buds are starting to swell, some showing their first leaves.

During this month, I prune ever-blooming modern roses such as hybrid teas, floribundas, grandifloras, polyanthas, and miniature roses. From the old garden rose collections I prune two classes: hybrid perpetuals and Portland roses.

In March, we can still get a cold spell, even snow. If this happens while I'm still pruning, I'm not overly concerned. Besides making it inconvenient for pruning, the snow is going to do little damage. It's later on, after pruning is done, that I'm concerned about dieback—once the buds have started to grow as a result of pruning.

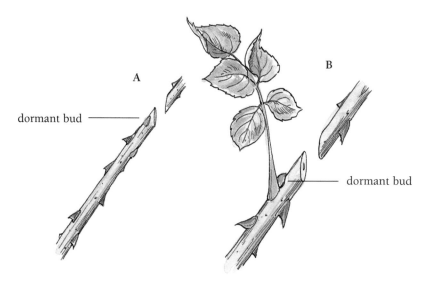

*Remember this simple pruning rule: always cut on an angle with the dormant bud at the top of the angle. This is true both for spring pruning (A) and during the growing season (B).*

Despite the threat of snow or sudden, late freezes, the pruning has to get done, so I move ahead with it. The botanical clock of these roses is ticking loudly as the days get longer and the sun warmer. By mid-March you should start seeing growth among these roses, whether or not you've pruned them.

To prevent all of the plant's stored nutrients from going to the smallest and weakest growing buds, I make sure that I'm out there pruning, despite the temperature, by Saint Patrick's Day. If you go out to plant your peas on the day of the green, you should be well into pruning your hybrid teas. **That's a rule I like to follow.**

Here's a quick review of the roses I select for pruning in March.

# OLD GARDEN ROSES

### PORTLAND
One of the classic arguments in the rose world revolves around the true identity of a rose often sold as 'Jacques Cartier'. Recently this pink beauty was renamed 'Marchesa Boccella', possibly our first rose to undergo a sex change (although at the moment there is a rumor that 'Mme. Boll' has been masquerading as the 'Comte de Chambord').

These are Portland roses (sometimes given the class name of damask perpetuals), important stepping-stones to the development of the hybrid tea class. The true origins of the Portland rose class and its individual members are vague—the subject of which will ignite the hottest arguments among rose collectors. What we do know is that the ever-blooming characteristic of these nineteenth-century roses comes from the China rose class, which explains their eagerness to grow at the first sign of spring.

There are a handful of these once popular roses sold today. Among them are 'Marchesa Boccella' (au revoir, Jacques), 'Rose de Rescht', and 'Rose du Roi'—three of the most popular cultivars today. Not only are they attractive garden shrubs with an upright and spreading habit, they are truly ever-blooming. Their all too brief moment of fame in the nineteenth century gave way to a new generation of roses known as hybrid perpetuals. A Portland was instrumental in producing the first of the large flowered hybrid perpetual class, the rage of the Victorian age.

### HYBRID PERPETUAL ROSES
Hybrid perpetuals gained in popularity quickly. These mutts of the rose world (they were a mix of just about every kind of rose growing in the Victorian garden) evolved into gangly, disease-ridden shrubs that produced large flowers. These blooms, displayed in English boxes (velvet-covered wood, with holes popped out, big enough to show the flower alone) were winning top prizes at the local flower shows, a new competitive sport among the gentlemen gardeners of this time. It seems that little attention was being paid to the growth habit; everything seemed to be focused on producing large and fragrant blooms. It's more than coincidence that horticulture journals of this time period were beginning to be inundated with articles and requests dealing with the problems of leaf spot, plant lice, and red spiders—now all too common rose ailments.

In climates with long, cool, growing seasons, these roses are truly perpetual blooming. For me, these roses give a flush of blooms at the beginning of the season and again near the end (this repeat bloom is only limited to a *very* small group).

Their habits vary. Some hybrid perpetuals are tidy, upright shrubs with twiggy growth. Others are vigorous growers, sending out arching canes of various lengths and capable of being used as climbers. Almost all of them produce their best blooms on very short side shoots coming off the older wood.

Hybrid perpetuals and Portlands both bloom on old wood (canes from pervious years) and new growth (canes that develop during this season). With this in mind, don't be afraid to cut—whatever grows should produce roses. After thinning center clutter, make sure that all branches have been shortened, even by just having their tips cut.

As with climbing roses, grab hold of each long cane and shorten all of the side shoots to a length of a few inches.

Portlands are easier to shape; as they age they develop a more graceful form. Hybrid perpetuals are more challenging.

Many of the long-limbed hybrid perpetuals should be trained into place. One interesting fashion is to peg them. Pegging requires a great deal of space for its best effect. After pruning, spread the canes outward, away from the center of the plant, as close as possible to the ground. A tent peg that is driven into the ground over the cane will hold these canes in place. Many garden centers sell pins used for holding landscape cloth (a type of

*Pegging a rose means to simply secure the longest canes directly into the ground with a wooden clothespin or a tent peg.*

*An unusual, but interesting, way of training a shrub or a climber into a mounding habit is to build a triangular corral-like structure around the plant. Secure the canes to the structure.*

mulch I don't recommend) in place. These would work as well. Side shoots loaded with new roses will grow all along the entire length of these pegged canes. The effect could be as beautiful as a carpet of roses.

Pegging can also be done with some of the Portlands. One in particular is "MacGregor's Damask" (for a discussion on this name, see **July**). A slight variation would be to peg only the older wood, allowing the newer canes to grow up and over the pegged canes. The result is a "skirt" type design around the newer growth.

Another style—rather than pegging the canes directly into the ground—is to build a low-lying fence around the shrub and tie outer canes of the rosebush to this structure. I can best describe this as building a corral around the rosebush. You can use a number of materials—wire, wood, or metal. Don't be too particular about your choice of materials; whatever you use will soon disappear, as it becomes covered in lax canes full of roses.

These designs can be done with *any* long-limbed rose with pliable canes, not just hybrid perpetual or Portland roses. Like climbing roses, an abundance of blooms will be produced whenever the canes are trained into a horizontal position.

Here's another interesting method for using hybrid perpetuals in the garden, one that I've only seen in French gardens. The hybrid perpetuals (in this case, the cultivar I admired was 'Mrs. John Laing') are planted near the edge of the garden. The longest canes are trained, horizontally, to a low wire that is strung along the border of the garden and the walk. The result is a low, fragrant fence, edging the garden.

# Modern Roses

### HYBRID TEA ROSES

Gardeners who prefer large, single-stemmed roses (just like the ones at the local florist) that bloom through the season should grow hybrid tea roses. 'La France', **considered by some to be the first hybrid tea rose**, was a true hybrid of a tea rose, as the name of the class implies. Born in 1867, 'La France' was the offspring of a tea rose and a hybrid perpetual. This original parentage was true for many of the earliest hybrid teas, right up through the early twentieth century. Today, hybrid teas such as 'Peace', 'Oklahoma', 'Jadis', and countless others are very far removed from the original prototype. Of various class influences, it seems that today, in order to be a hybrid tea, the only qualification is that the blooms be large and held on long stems (hmm, but some modern hybrid teas now even come in clustered forms!).

To refer to a hybrid tea as simply a **tea** rose is incorrect and very confusing. These are two different rose classes, each requiring a different approach to pruning (not to mention the climate limitation on tea roses). The word "hybrid" is the important key to their differences. (see **April** for more on tea roses.)

It's been over one hundred years since 'La France' introduced the first of the modern rose classes. Thousands of new hybrid teas have been created, and more will be in the future. This is the most popular class of roses ever produced. And, probably the most dreaded when it comes to pruning.

Many hybrid tea roses take a beating in the winter, dying back sometimes to the ground. It's frightening to prune one of these winter-damaged roses. By the time you have removed just deadwood, there isn't much else left. This is Mother Nature's pruning at its best, and she's teaching us a valuable lesson. It doesn't hurt to be severe with hybrid teas when you are pruning. But I have to admit it's much easier to this after having experienced this terror.

The first time I pruned hybrid tea roses, all I left behind were stubby canes and bud unions—and that was just removing deadwood (these roses had been in poor health). I figured I had pretty much rid the garden of hybrid teas and I wouldn't have a job much longer. But, luckily for me, hybrid teas are not as fragile as they seem. This rigorous pruning exercise resulted in a beautiful display of roses that very June—all of the blooms on healthy new wood growing from the bud union.

Follow all of the basic steps to pruning, discussed earlier in the year! With hybrid teas, apart from removing as much clutter of dead and thin branches as possible, the emphasis will be on shortening and thinning the shrub to *a few select* sturdy canes.

Decide on the height you want in your garden. Hybrid teas don't have to be cut to a standard height—it's what works best for your garden and what you feel most comfortable with.

If you are working in a bed with many plants of the same cultivar planted together, then keep in mind that the display of roses will look better if the plants are pruned to a similar height. If you have one or two in a mixed-flower border, or the hybrid tea is standing alone, then the final height is whatever you think looks best for the rest of the border.

Whatever you decide, keep the following in mind: Hybrid tea roses pruned very short will take a little bit longer to come into bloom than those left higher. However, the plant that is pruned closer to the ground will produce the largest roses.

## FLORIBUNDA, GRANDIFLORA

Sprays of roses are typical of floribundas: clusters of blooms held high above the plants of medium height. It was during the 1930's that this unique style of rosebush was noticed among the new shrubs coming from breeding programs at major rose nurseries. 'Smiles', a clustered flowered pink rose, was introduced in 1939 as the first official floribunda.

Popular as bedding plants, these reliable repeat bloomers quickly found their way to all gardens. This wasn't the end of the evolution of the clustered flowered rose, however. In 1954, a tall-growing and large-flowered version of a floribunda was introduced with the name 'Queen Elizabeth'. The flowers were of hybrid tea size, but still displayed in clusters. It was decided to create a new class, grandiflora, for this type of rose.

For the longest time, the British rose society had the right idea: They didn't recognize any of these modern class names of American origin (hybrid tea, floribunda, grandiflora). They found it way to confusing. Instead, they categorized these new hybrids as clustered flowered and non-clustered flowered roses. Oh, that was so much easier to understand! Today, however, the class names hybrid tea, floribunda, and grandiflora are recognized (though not entirely accepted) throughout the world.

Experiments have been done with pruning the floribundas and grandifloras using hedge shears. The results were promising, except that after several seasons of shearing there was still a need to remove the clutter of

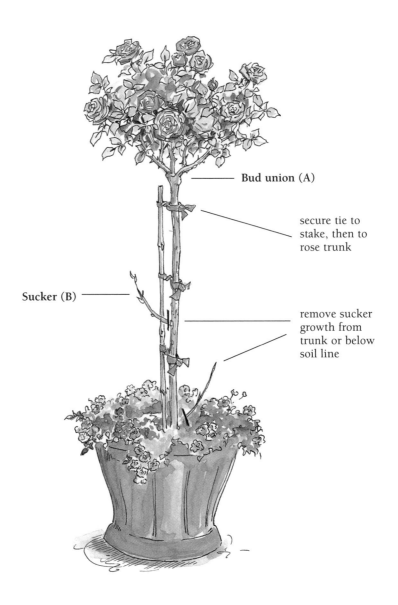

Bud union (A)

secure tie to stake, then to rose trunk

Sucker (B)

remove sucker growth from trunk or below soil line

*Just about any class of rose is available as a standard, or tree form, style. The most common classes used are hybrid tea and floribunda roses. A tree rose is created by grafting the "pretty" rose high up on a stem of a vigorous rootstock. Prune the top part as you would a regular bush form of the rose. Any growth (B) below the bud union (A) should be removed. (See **June** for more on suckering.)*

twiggy wood and deadwood from the center of the plants. But this time it was only much denser. A thorough, more traditional style of pruning was eventually needed to clean up the plants. I still prefer, and recommend, becoming intimate with the shrubs every spring and more involved in shaping the plants through careful pruning.

Select your height, again depending on how and where you are using your plants in the garden. For the quickest and fullest bedding display, leave many thin canes intact. If you want larger flowers, then cut back all the canes above a bud eye where the canes are the thickness of a number 2 pencil. In general, leave behind as much wood as you can without creating a crowded situation.

## POLYANTHA ROSES

Polyanthas were popular during the late Victorian era and into the early twentieth century as buttonhole roses. In the garden they produced small roses in clustered arrangements on low-growing plants. It was the further development of these small flowered roses that led to the first floribundas. **Polyanthas are still very popular today as garden plants.**

Personally, when it comees to pruning, I would rather let an enthusiastic volunteer struggle with these short and twiggy shrubs.

One year a rabbit had gnawed completely around the stem of one of my 'Mlle. Cécile Brunner' roses (probably one of the most famous polyanthas ever created), killing the top part of the plant. I had no choice but to cut the entire top part off, **right down to the ground level.** My reward for this severe pruning was a fantastic display of larger than usual pink sweetheart roses, **all** on new growth from the base of the plant, all summer.

The choice is yours—be ruthless, or pick and choose. **Either technique works with these small flowered roses.** You can get tired real fast of the twiggy growth of polyanthas—but that's all they do. Careful pruning will reward you with a very attractive plant, as well as beautiful flowers. Or, you could just wait for a hungry rabbit.

## MINIATURE ROSES

If you thought the polys (rosarian-speak for polyanthas) were twiggy, how about pruning a miniature rose? I wouldn't recommend saving this job for the end of the day. Sometimes, if you're lucky, the rabbits will have pruned these for you, too.

Miniature roses are the smallest growing of all the everblooming modern roses. They have small everything: flowers, leaves, buds—even little prickles. (**Caution: They may be small, but they still draw blood!**)

As with their bigger cousins, cluttered growth will only invite problems later in the season. They should be thinned, uncluttered, and shortened—the height is variable. It's difficult sometimes to find the **bud eyes**. I just guess, cut, then wait and see; it's the best method, short of using a magnifying glass. You'll need a great deal of patience for this minute pruning, thin scissors (I use a pair of scissors that was actually sold for cutting chicken skins), and a soft cushion.

While all of this pruning is going on in March, I leave the gates open for visitors who want to see how the pruning is done and ask questions. The ones with too many questions are handed a pair of pruning shears (I keep several spares handy for that reason).

Those who remember the beauty of the previous season are shocked, or even saddened by the appearance of the pruned garden. I don't think they truly believe me when I reassure them that the garden will be in full bloom in just three months (during my first spring, I didn't believe it, either!)

Pruning is a meditative process. Why rush through it? You can learn a great deal about your roses and your garden while you're on a close encounter with your plants. Look at the plants, examine their growth habits. Take this time to get to know the intimate details of your rosebushes. You won't see them this way again—and from this perspective-until next year.

Study the conditions of your canes and **examine them for any signs of pests**. This is an important step for preventing the spread of diseases and insects that could infect or infest your plant at epidemic proportions in only a few months' time. Think prevention: Deal with the problems before you see them. Removing crowded canes, deadwood, and damaged canes during pruning is the first step to managing pests in your rose garden.

This is especially important if you have had bad luck in previous years with **black spot, powdery mildew, downy mildew,** or **rust**. These diseases over-winter in the form of spores on the canes—either in wounds, around the emerging leaf buds, in deadwood, or even around the bases of the prickles. Each of these problems will be discussed individually in upcoming months.

Whether you've had a problem or not with these diseases, I recommend spraying your rose garden with **lime-sulfur** when you're done with the pruning. If lime-sulfur is unavailable in your area, try a garden sulfur spray instead. These sprays will kill over-wintered fungal spores. Lime-sulfur also controls the spread of **canker**, another fungal disease that is easy to spot but just as easy to miss. You can't miss it while pruning. So get down there and take a closer look.

There are many types of canker: Look for a lesion or discoloration on any cane. Lesions can vary in ugliness, from discolored concentric rings to irregular blotches, and are always visible on the surface of the canes. It's perfectly normal for a rosebush to have purple or red canes, and even some uneven coloration. I've noticed among some roses that the sides of canes exposed to the winter sun show a discoloration—sort of like a sunburn. This is not canker. Canker lesions are very different, more like a stain on the stem.

If you've just purchased an old house with a garden full of old rose plants that have been neglected for a very long time, be prepared. None of the canes will look picture-perfect. In fact, it might appear that the roses are overwhelmed with canker. It's very likely that the canes are just so old that the original color of the stem has turned to gray, so don't panic.

Sometimes you will encounter old wounds on your canes. These could fool you into thinking you have canker. Rabbit or other animal damage can be mistaken for disease, too. If you're not sure, wait and see. As the plant begins to grow, canker lesions will increase and eventually girdle the cane that it has infected. The danger of waiting, however, is that you can lose an entire plant to this disease.

Canes that are infected with canker tend to have a lack of substance to them. If you cut through an area with a lesion, the inside tissue will not be firm like a healthy cane should be.

It's also easy to miss a lesion. For this reason I always try looking at the pruned rosebush from a different angle, or come back to it in a few weeks for a fresh inspection.

Cankers can readily infect the plant through wounds in the stems and through any stubs left behind during pruning. This is one of the reasons that it is extremely important to cut canes as close as possible to a dormant bud whenever you prune.

If your plant is overtaken with canker, then cut the entire plant to the bud union. The other alternative would be to shovel-prune it; that is, toss the plant out!

Fungal diseases are spread by spores that move from plant to plant by way of water. You can also easily *carry* spores from one plant to another—or from one garden to another, while pruning or simply by brushing up against an infected plant.

The spread of canker and other diseases can be curbed by cleaning your tools between the pruning of each individual rosebush. Get into a routine that includes wiping pruners with a rag infused with alcohol as you go from plant to plant. Another practice that helps prevent the accidental spread of fungal disease is to avoid pruning while the roses are wet.

**Crown gall** is a disease caused by bacteria. It's very easy to spot crown gall and rid your garden of it at pruning time. Crown gall is a growth that resembles a cauliflower growing on stems or around canes at the soil level (the crown of your rose), as well as higher up on the stems (for **root gall**, see **August**). This infection can eventually kill a plant if left unchecked, and can spread to other plants through pruning and by way of the soil. It is not as common as canker, but it pays to be always on the lookout for it. Gall is especially infectious as the soil warms up. Gardeners in warm climates should be very careful to check for this disease on a regular basis.

If you see gall on your plant, remove it. It's as simple as that. Make sure that you clean your tools with alcohol or a bleach solution immediately after cutting the gall from the bush. If I spot a gall growing on a rose, and I haven't pruned it yet, I wait until I've pruned all the healthy plants first before pruning the infected one.

Years ago the practice was to throw away the infected plant. Today, this is not necessary. If the growth is small, gall can be stopped from reoccurring. After removing the growth, swab the infected area with an antibacterial ointment (such as you would use for a wound on your skin). If the gall has completely engulfed the base of the plant, then I would shovel-prune the rose.

Watch for insects as you prune your roses. Two in particular that are difficult to see unless you are on your hands and knees cutting are **scale** (see **February**) and **rose cane borer.**

As you prune from bush to bush be on the lookout for what resembles a drilled hole down the center of the rose canes. This perfectly round tunnel is just that—a tunnel created by the larval form of an insect. Rosarians often generalize when referring to this culprit by calling it "rose cane borer." The truth is that many different pests masquarade under the guise of rose can borer. The majority of the tunneling is done by larvae of any number of insects, but most commonly **sawflies.** Sawflies are discussed in detail in **June**, when they do their most damage during the first flush of bloom.

There are two other possible culprits: one is the **small carpenter bee**, and the other is the annoying **leafcutting bee** (more on this pest in **June**). Both use the canes of your rosebush as a nest and food source for their developing larvae and also as a winter nest.

Whatever the true identity of the larva, borer is an apt description and it's the larva forms that do the most damage. The insect bores its way downward through the rose cane, hibernating inside the canes all winter. As the early spring sun warms the canes, the larva will feed some more onto the cane, mature and fly away to continue the cycle elsewhere (hopefully in your neighbor's rose garden!). Sometimes a cane that has (or had) a borer in it will have a strip of scar tissue running the length of the bore-hole on the outside of the cane.

To control these critters, cut the cane with the borehole. Start cutting at the top and work your way down until you have completely removed all signs of the borer. Sometimes, you could be removing last year's home. But if you're lucky, you'll encounter the small white larva in its cozy nest. Destroy the worm: A snip or a "smoosh" is all you need.

No doubt there are insecticides (chemicals used to kill insects) that can be used to kill borers. I have never considered using chemicals to control bores, nor will I ever. Don't waste your money or your health. Try some safe preventative measures instead.

**If you find that your garden is prone to rose cane borer, here are much safer options to consider.** It's much easier, and more effective, to dab all of the cut canes with a white glue, such as Elmer's Glue-All. I have heard of gardeners using nail polish to cover pruning cuts. For those who have always suspected that gardening and nail polish are incompatible, consider: Have you ever had to sit on a city bus while the person next to you is painting their nails? Something that smells that bad can't possibly be good for the roses!

My aunt Joanne in New Jersey had a practical and colorful remedy for preventing rose cane borer. She would dab all of the cuts of her climbing rose with her favorite red lipstick (I have a clouded memory of her wearing her fur coat as she did this!). I often wondered if it was significant that the lipstick was the same color as the roses. The lipstick was "Love That Red," the rose was the red climber 'Blaze'.

A sight welcome in every garden, and often spotted during pruning, are signs of the friendly praying mantis. You might not even know you have these insects in your garden until now, since they blend in so effectively with the foliage of the roses during the growing season.

My respect for these mate eaters goes way back. I can remember as a kid being warned by my big brothers that the police would arrest me is I was ever caught killing a praying mantis!

Praying mantis, along with ladybugs, are the sacred cows of the rose garden: They feed on aphids and other juicy garden pests. While pruning, you might come across an egg case or two. They resemble a piece of brown foam attached to a rose cane. If you need to cut this cane, save the nest. Maybe hang it in a safe corner in your garden. You can't have too many praying mantises is your garden.

In addition to inspecting for diseases and insects in your garden while pruning, remove any plants that didn't survive the winter. Or if the plant is alive but you want to move it, this is a good time to do that (transplanting will be covered in **November**).

Pruning signals the beginning of the growing season, the start of spring. Healthy plants should have enough energy stored from last season to get started. However, roses are fast growers, requiring lots of nutrients to grow and bloom. They benefit enormously from additional nutrients in the form of fertilizer (often referred to as "rose food"). I begin my fertilizing program once I finish pruning. Whether you garden in Seattle, Tampa, or Boston, this is a good rule for you to follow, too.

Easy does it with the fertilizers! Lots of things can go wrong if you use too much. An overdose can cause a great deal of damage—immediate and long lasting. One of the guaranteed ways of attracting bad insects and diseases to your garden is to over fertilize. This causes excess succulent growth—prime real estate for a homeless aphid.

Whether this is your first time growing roses or you are a seasoned rosarian, you should have a complete soil analysis of your soil done—ideally every year. Before you add any fertilizer to your garden, find out what you need. Let your soil profile dictate how much and what type of fertilizer you should be using, not someone who is trying to sell you "rose food."

You can put down all of the fertilizers available, but unless the soil is at the proper pH, you will be wasting your time and money. When the soil pH isn't right, the nutrients can be "locked" out, because the soil will not release the nutrients to the plant. You need to have your soil pH checked annually: The ideal pH for roses is 5.6—6.6. Kits for measuring pH are available at most garden centers.

Soil profiles, on the other hand, are a bit more involved. Most agricultural extension agents (usually a service provided by the local agricultural college) for a small fee. This might seem like an inconvenience, but it really is quite simple and well worth the effort. You will find out exactly what is in your soil and what is lacking. Do this before you spend a great deal of money on fertilizer. It wouldn't hurt to have your soil tested every year, or at least ever other year.

Annual soil profiles for the Cranford Rose Garden have shown that each month I need to apply to an average-sized rosebush approximately 1 cup (a handful) of a fertilizer with the nutrient ratio of 10-6-4. This high nitrogen fertilizer is actually sold as a lawn fertilizer. It comes in a 50 percent organic form, including trace elements (more on trace elements in **May**).

All fertilizers come in labeled packages telling you exactly what is inside and what the fertilizer is derived from. Nitrogen, phosphorous, and potassium are the essential nutrients required for the healthy growth of all plants—including roses—and on the package are three numbers that are important to understand. These numbers represent the nutrient ratio for the particular fertilizer package you are looking at. The three numbers indicate the percentage of each nutrient in the fertilizer. For example, the 40-pound bag of fertilizer I use has the numbers 10-6-4. That means that in this particular bag, **10 percent** of the forty pounds is **nitrogen, 6 percent** of the package is **phosphorous,** and **4 percent** is **potassium.** The remaining 80 percent of the bag is filler, possibly also containing trace elements.

Which ratio and how much you should use will vary greatly depending on where you garden and what type of soil you grow your roses in. I can't overstress the importance of having a soil profile so that you will always know exactly what you are dealing with.

Here is a brief breakdown of the benefits of the three main ingredients of a fertilizer:

- **N (nitrogen)**—gives natural dark green color to foliage; stimulates and increases leaf and stem growth
- **P (phosphorus)**—is important for root growth; gives plants a vigorous start; provides strength and hardiness
- **K (potassium)**—converts to potash; builds up disease resistance; yields strong flower stalks; increases the numbers of flowers.

Chemical fertilizers are man-made and contain these necessary components that the plant needs to grow in a ready-to-use fashion. These types of fertilizers deliver the goods quickly to the plant, sort of like fast food for roses.

Chemical fertilizers, also referred to as inorganic, come in both granular forms (grains that you work into the soil) and a water-soluble form (needs to be mixed with water and either poured around the plant or sprayed onto the foliage).

After pruning, and before the plants have begun to grow, the best type of chemical fertilizer to use is a granular form. I apply 10-6-4 now to all of my established roses (not the newly planted ones). I repeat the ¹/₄ cup per bush each month with the ever-blooming roses only, continuing right through the summer and stopping after August. With the once blooming roses, I repeat the ¹/₄ only once after they have bloomed.

If you pour all of your fertilizer onto one spot or up against the rose canes, you could have trouble (leave a tiny pile on the lawn and you'll see what fertilizer burn looks like). Here's the correct way to apply a granular fertilizer: With gloved-hands, broadcast—or scatter—the grains between the rows of roses, or make a wide circle around each plant to avoid getting the grains on any plant parts. Then gently work the fertilizer into the top layers of the soil.

Water the garden thoroughly *before* and *after* applying granular fertilizers. If you don't water, you could end up with fertilizer burn. These fertilizers are salts. If they sit around the roots of the roses, and the soil is dry, they will draw moisture out of the plants, resulting in brown edges to the leaves for a burned appearance.

With this in mind, I eventually adjusted my fertilizing schedule in the Cranford Rose Garden. The soil profile recommended 1 full cup of fertilizer at each application. I ended up reducing this to $1/4$ of a cup (a small handful). I felt that this was a safer amount, not a very strong dose of fertilizer at one time. I started this change once I began to pay attention to the health of the garden soil and became more interested in the use of organic fertilizers. Organic fertilizers are really much better for your roses, and the garden as well.

Organic fertilizers are more than fertilizers. They should be thought of as both a nutrient source and a soil conditioner. Coming entirely from natural sources, organics improve the quality of the soil, making it a better place for your roses to grow. A soil rich in organic substances will create lots of activity among friendly bacteria in the soil. These bacteria in turn release nutrients that are otherwise unavailable to the roots of the rosebush. Strong-growing root systems produce strong-growing, healthy roses.

Organic fertilizers are not fast-acting, so it can take time for the nutrients in the soil to be released. Start adding organics to your soil now. Organics work their best when the soil and air temperature are cool.

There are many different organic materials to consider for your garden; manure, compost, ashes, and wood chips are some of the most common. The nutrient content of organic fertilizers is not as concentrated as with inorganic fertilizers. Manure and blood meal are good nitrogen sources, bone meal is an easy source of phosphorous, and potash can be found in wood ash as well as in manure and mushroom compost.

Today there are many packaged organic fertilizers to be used (and they are usually very fragrant). In New Orleans, rosarians recommend an application of green sand (a naturally occurring sediment and an excellent source of potash and iron), 1 cup per plant annually after spring pruning. I have had great success with a packaged organic that is made up of bone meal, blood meal, alfalfa meal, cottonseed meal, and fish meal. I use this twice a year as a supplement to my application of 10-6-4. I put down some now and again after the first blooms have faded. The amounts to use vary from product to product. Although you can use some organic fertilizers as frequently as on a monthly basis, always follow the instructions on the package.

Those of you who are still enjoying the benefits of Mother Nature's white precipitate mulch (snow)—don't become impatient. In the next month you should be able to get out there and start pruning and bleeding like the rest of us. If you're in the warmer regions of the country, this is just about your last call for planting bare-root roses.

If you're in a warm climate and you've planted cool weather annuals such as petunias, nemesia, and violas as winter companions for your roses, you may want to freshen these up with a little bit of shearing as well. In my northern garden I try violas for winter color, sometimes they survive the freezes, often they don't. But I try to add them to the garden now to compliment the emerging foliage of the roses, to add color to the early spring garden, and to compliment the spring flowering bulbs that will be emerging very shortly. I always under plant my roses with a variety of spring bulbs (see **November**).

Now that my pruning is nearly finished (I still have those tender varieties to do in April), I'm going to prepare for the arrival of my bare-root roses. April is the month for planting.

---

## ORGANIC SOURCES
- **Nitrogen (N):** alfalfa pellets, blood meal, fish emulsion, seaweed, manure, cottonseed meal, fish meal, coffee grounds, soybean meal, compost
- **Phosphate (P):** colloidal phosphate, bone meal, guano, manure
- **Potassium (K):** greensand, kelp meal, wood ashes, banana skins, granite dust, manure

## RECOMMENDED MEMBERSHIP
Heritage Rose Foundation
- A non-profit organization whose goal is to collect and preserve heritage roses and promote their culture.
- Membership includes a subscription to *Rosa Mundi: Journal of the Heritage Rose Foundation*. Published three times a year.

**For more information and to subscribe:**
Heritage Rose Foundation
PO Box 831414
Richardson, TX  75083
Website: **www.heritagerosefoundation.org**
Various membership levels are offered

## RECOMMENDED READING
*The Organic Rose Garden.* Liz Druitt. Dallas, TX: Taylor Publishing, 1996

## ROSE CLASSES

This is a basic list of the most important rose classes from which there are many beautiful rose varieties and cultivars to choose from:

- *Old Garden Roses:* species, species hybrids, gallicas, damasks, albas, centifolias, mosses, Chinas, teas, Noisettes, Bourbons, hybrid Bourbons, hybrid Noisettes, hybrid Chinas, Portlands, hybrid perpetuals
- *Modern Roses:* hybrid teas, polyanthas, floribundas, grandifloras, miniatures, climbers, ramblers, shrubs, hybrid musks, hybrid rugosas

## WINTER/EARLY SPRING ANNUALS AS COMPANIONS

Violas and pansies
Nemesia
Species petunias
Lobelia
Stock
Snapdragons
Annual phlox

## COMPANIONS TO CONSIDER

**Vines:**
*Annual*
    Moonflower (*Ipomea alba*)
    Morning Glory
    Cigar Vine (*Manetia lutea-rusia*)
*Perennial*
    Clematis
    Chocolate Vine (*Akebia quinata*)
    Gloriosa Lily (*Gloriosa superba* 'Rothschildiana')
*Woody*
    Wisteria
    Climbing Hydrangea

# APRIL

Cruelly, it's often a rainy, cold spring afternoon when the UPS delivery leaves a box marked LIVE PLANTS/OPEN IMMEDIATELY (April showers. . .). But I rip open the package and wade through the plastic and wet newspaper shreds to find buried treasure. Squeezed into that box, measuring 2$^1$/$_2$ feet long by 1 foot high and wide are ten **bare-root roses** I ordered in January. They look like anything *but* rosebushes: long brown roots all entangled together, and thick greenish-red, prickly sticks with no signs of life (except for the swollen, pale green buds all over the stems). Is this really a climber? I think to myself as I hold up a plant that has canes all of 10 inches tall. As I unwrap the packing material, I can see that all of the plants in this box are the same size. If it weren't for the name tags attached, it would be next to impossible to tell the hybrid teas from the English roses, or old roses from modern. At this stage they all look alike: muddy and ugly.

Never mind daffodils or blooming magnolias; for me, the harbinger of spring is the arrival of bare-root roses. These are dormant plants, ready to grow. From the moment I open the box, they have become my responsibility. April's the month for planting roses.

Bare-root roses that arrive now need to be planted as soon as possible. Warm temperatures can start them growing, whether or not the plant is in the ground. So the first think to do is to keep the new plants cool and moist from immediately upon their arrival until you're ready to plant. If you can't plant them right away, the next best thing is to bring them out to the garden and heel them in until planting time.

**Heeling in** is an outdoor storage technique—basically a temporary planting. You can store the roses in the bed that they are intended for, or perhaps in the vegetable patch, the compost pile, a soil pile, or any open area of the garden where you can dig a shallow trench. Put the bundles of roses into the trench (roots first!), and backfill with loose soil over all of the roots and as much of the bundle as you can. Leave at least a small portion of the tops of the roses exposed, and maybe a piece of bright landscape ribbon attached to one of the canes. This is so that you won't forget where they are. I've often fond the backsides of my compost pile dotted with beautiful roses in June!

Unless you garden in a zone where the ground is frozen solid or there's a good chance of temperatures plunging into single digits, don't be over concerned that it's too cold for the new roses. Having been stored for months in temperatures near freezing, these bare-root roses are acclimated to the cold. If you've heeled them in and a freeze is in the forecast, cover them entirely with some mulch (don't forget to mark their location).

Another alternative is to leave them in the box. But, you should at least take a look to make sure that the nursery did indeed send you what you asked for. **Each plant should be labeled.** As you're doing inventory, check the grade (see **January**) and also prune off blackened and mushy canes—these are dead. Never hesitate to call a nursery to complain (or compliment them) about the quality of the plants you've received.

After you've opened the box and checked the plants, rewrap the roots and the tops of the plants in damp (not dripping) newspaper. Put the plants back in the plastic wrap and close the box. **Store the box in the coolest possible place, away from any heat, and especially out of the sun.** It's important to check the roses periodically to make sure that the roots are continually moist during storage.

A final alternative, and the most space consuming, would be to plant the roses in **pots**. If you decide to pot them up, keep them in cool storage or place outside in the sun, if possible. I have an old open cistern attached to my house. This 4-foot pit serves as an excellent place to store my early arrivals either potted up or bare-rooted. I wouldn't recommend trying to grow these potted roses indoors—this could be too difficult a task (see **December**).

Roses shipped to you in pots can be left in the pots they arrive in, but in sunlight. Don't be shocked by the condition of these plants when you open the box. It is very possible that these roses can be in full leaf, in bloom (very common with miniature roses), or dead looking. As recently as the day before they were shipped, it was likely that these roses were in full leaf and in bloom. Some nurseries will send them that way; others strip the plants of their beauty before packing for shipping. Since these roses are no longer dormant, it would be a good idea to put them in the sun as soon as possible. **A good rule is to not order potted roses until you know they can go right into the garden or a good place to grow.** Most nurseries will ship to you at the proper time for planting in your area.

Unless the canes are black and mushy, the rose is very much alive. However, due to the fact that these plants just spent more than a few days inside a box it's very likely that yellow leaves and even mold will greet you. Get the plants out of the box and into a sunny spot. Clean all debris from the pots, then prune all damaged and dead wood. Prune any crowded canes to give new growth a chance to form a desirable shape.

**Miniature roses** are often shipped in full leaf and bloom—a wonderful way to receive them. One problem with this is that the pots these little roses are growing in are too small for a long-lasting display. Move the roses into bigger pots (at least 6 inches in diameter) or directly into the ground. If you leave them in the smaller pots, their leaves will start to yellow and fall off.

Often many large size roses, usually own-root roses, are shipped in small pots, called **liners**. These, too, should be re-potted into bigger pots before going into the garden. In cold climates, it's actually a good idea to keep these roses in the larger pots until they have established a stronger root system. Start with a 6-inch or 12-inch pot. Once the new rose has become well rooted in the larger pot, it should be ready for your garden.

The best thing for every newly arrived rose is to plant it as soon as possible in its permanent place, whether it be in the ground or in a large container. Potted roses that are arriving from the south, from California, from the Pacific Northwest, or from a greenhouse should not be put into the garden until all threats of a killing frost have passed.

**The ideal planting time for roses will vary depending on which region of the country you garden in and your local weather conditions.** But wherever you are, whether you plant your roses in the ground or in containers high on tops of tall buildings, the general rule to follow is that a rose can be planted whenever the ground isn't frozen, and when there's no imminent danger of a severe freeze (or heat wave, too!). However, from Anchorage, Alaska, to Miami, Florida, *the way to plant* a rose and the *basic requirements* needed to grow roses are the same.

Roses need sunlight, at least five hours each day. The number one reason why a rosebush does not bloom is because there isn't enough sunlight. Morning sun, midday, afternoon sun, or all-day sun are your choices. In cooler climates, sunshine all day is best, while in hotter climates roses benefit greatly from a cooling afternoon shade. Roses will not bloom in dense shade, and roses growing in shadier parts of the garden will be especially prone to foliage diseases.

Regular watering is essential to maintaining a healthy rose plant, so long as the roses are growing in well-drained soil. There are only a few roses that will tolerate boggy conditions, and these belong to a species class. One of these, *Rosa palustris,* is a native and great for attracting birds to your garden. Cultivated garden roses will only languish in soggy situations. I have seen many roses die because they were planted in areas where water collected. If they don't drown during the growing season, they will surely perish once their roots are frozen in ice over the winter.

Before planting, the first thing I do to asses a site for roses is push a spading fork into the soil with all my weight. If it penetrates easily, I plant. If it hits hardpan (a hard-to-penetrate layer of soil), large rocks, or the handle breaks, I may want to consider another spot—or amend the site I have. Roses need **friable soil**—a soil containing a generous amount of particle matter, and that is easy to break up. In this type of soil, air passes through freely and water percolate at a rate slow enough to allow the roots to absorb the nutrients from the soil.

The friable natures of different soils are as various as the soil types themselves that are found throughout the country. Hold some soil in your hand and work your fingers through it. Notice if it's granular or silt-like. It should smell fresh, not rancid. Beyond this tactile inspection, there's as simple experiment you can conduct in your garden to determine how fast, or slowly, the water passes through your soil.

**To do this test, all you'll need are two coffee cans with their tops and bottoms removed and enough water to fill the cans:**
The day before, remove any large obstructions (surface sticks, stones, or leaves) from the area you are going to test and soak the area well. On the following day, push one coffee can into the soil, about 2 inches deep. Nearby, in the same moistened area, dig a hole about 18 inches deep and push the other coffee can into the soil at the bottom of this hole. Fill both canes to their tops with water. Record how long it takes for the water level, in both cans, to drop an inch.

The ideal soil draining time for roses is about 1 inch per hour. This is the rate for a standard sandy-loam mix (sand with a soil containing lots of organic matter). Pure sand will drain too quickly for adequate nutrient absorption, and pure clay can drain as slowly as .02 inches per hour, sometimes even taking as long as five days to completely drain.

An important addition to correct the drainage of your soil is an **organic ingredient**. This can be one of many things: decomposed leaves, manure, wood chips, or garden compost. Find out what's available locally.

Clay soils can be improved with horse manure, a week out of the horse with all the stable fixins'. Cow manure is best for sandy soils (maybe a month-or-two old (when it's not too sticky!). Otherwise, lots of bulky materials such as wood chips or leaf mold can greatly improve the quality of your soil.

Plant your roses away from the competing roots of large trees and shrubs. Roses do not fare well if they have to compete for their nutrients. Aggressive shrubs such as boxwoods and privets and large trees like maples will steal from your roses in no time at all. You need to keep the fast-growing roots of these shrubs in check with a sharp spade.

**A serious situation I have to deal with is the continual invasion of the roots of Norway maples.** The trees themselves are thirty feet away, but the roots have discovered the delicious soil in my border of old roses. Any rose that I plant in this bed suffers terribly. From digging in the beds, I've discovered that feeder roots from the trees have invaded the beds, severely restricting the growth of the roses. The trees refuse to fall during hurricanes (and I do keep my fingers crossed!).

Since I'm not handy with a chain saw, I'm following instead the advice of the Central Florida Heritage Rose Society. They recommend planting roses in 20-gallon pots (21 inches in diameter, 17 inches deep) and sinking the pots into the border[1]. In the warm climate of central Florida, the roses tend to outgrow the pots in a few seasons, and there is constant need for watering due to the heat. In the Northeast, I hope to be able to grow the roses for a longer time, even for a very long time, in these pots.

When I remember the pathetic-looking plants I'm trying to grow, I realize I have nothing to lose. One further tip: Be sure to leave a few inches of the pot above the soil level to prevent the tree roots from invading the pot at the surface level.

An update on this situation: Six years ago, in the spring of 2005, the last of the Norway maples were removed, due to old age (no, it wasn't a crazed rosarian with a chain saw). The roses in the submerged pots have been liberated and the entire border is flourishing. That's really good news, but all I can think about are the twenty holes—large holes—that I had to dig!

To prepare a bare-root rose for planting, hold the plant in one hand and orient yourself as to which way is up. One season I was called on a consultation to find that the gardener (I should say *ex*—gardener) had planted some of the roses upside down. In case you aren't sure, the long scraggly parts are the roots, and the stiff, often prickly parts are the stems.

Prune away any damaged or twiggy growth. Shorten remaining canes by at least 1/3 their length (always to an outward-facing bud, just as though you were spring pruning). The point is to make sure you cut all the canes, thereby signaling the plant to break its dormancy and begin to grow.

Trim the roots. Removing as much as half their length will encourage new fibrous root growth. Then immediately following this, soak the plants in muddy water containing fish emulsion (1 tablespoon per gallon of water) for at least four hours, and preferably over night. A large garbage can, deep enough to submerge the plants totally, would be perfect. If you have a pond or stream, that would work too—only tie the roses to the shore and skip the fish emulsion.

## PLANTING A BARE-ROOT ROSE BUSH
To plant a bare-root rose bush, follow these steps:
A. Trim the roots and canes of the bare-root rose
B. Soak the plant in a bucket of muddy water (or a solution of fish emulsion or manure tea) for at least four hours
C. The hole should be wide enough so that the root system fits without bending the roots. Put a mound of compost at the bottom of the hole
D. With the rose firmly in place, backfill the hole with a mix of soil and compost. Water thoroughly to saturate the entire system
E. With additional compost and soil, mound up around the canes of the newly planted rose to protect it from the drying heat of the sun.

Overcast, cool, calm, and even a bit misty would describe the perfect planting day. However, time is of the essence with bare-root roses, so if you can't arrange for this weather, at least keep the roses soaking and out of the sun until you are ready to plant them.

Dig a hole wider than the spread of the root system, enough so that you can place the roots in the hole without crowding or bending them. The hole should contain ample amounts of loose compost. Hold the plant firmly in place and backfill the hole with soil and compost, always pushing the soil mix in among all the roots, and thereby eliminating any hidden air pockets around the roots. As you gradually backfill the hole, use your hands, not your feet, to press the soil into place. Foot stomping will compact the soil. The final step before watering is to mound additional compost and soil up around the canes of the newly planted rose bush to protect it from the drying heat of the sun. I usually make my mounds about 6 to 8 inches high. Once the rose starts growing you can gently knock the mounds away.

The "magic" ingredients added to the planting holes are various. Human hair, grease drippings, waste materials from home breweries, and even old leather boots have been recommended through the centuries. Seasoned rose growers have been known to add a fish head or two to the hole and just endure the fragrance. Not I. However, bananas are a part of my daily diet, and two skins per hole are a natural source of potassium for my roses. In many small villages of France, it's still a tradition for good luck to plant a rose with your newborn child's placenta.

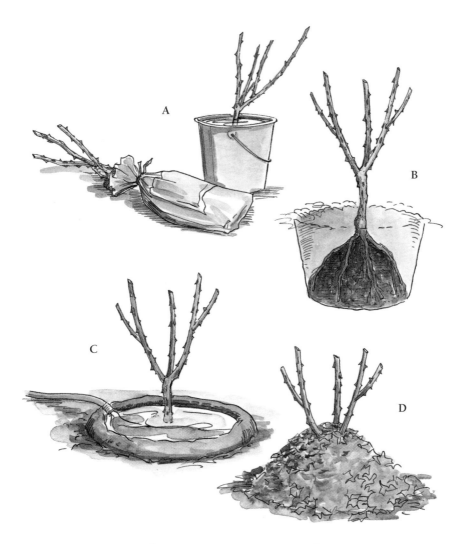

### Planting a Bare-root Rose Bush

**A** *Trim the roots and canes of the bare-root rose. Soak the plant in a bucket of muddy water (or a solution of fish emulsion or manure tea) for at least four hours.*

**B** *The hole should be wide enough so that the root system fits without bending the roots. Put a mound of compost at the bottom of the hole.*

**C** *With the rose firmly in place, backfill the hole with a mix of soil and compost. Water thoroughly to saturate the entire root system.*

**D** *With additional compost and soil, mound up around the canes of the newly planted rose to protect it from the drying heat of the sun.*

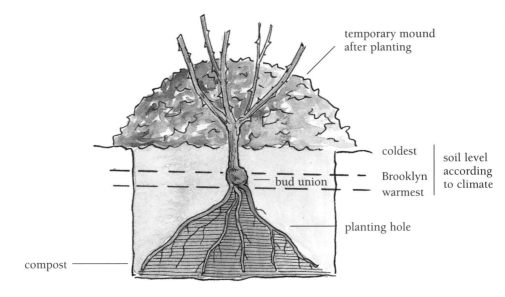

temporary mound
after planting

coldest

bud union

Brooklyn

warmest

soil level
according
to climate

planting hole

compost

*The colder the winters, the deeper you should position the bud union when planting.*

**If you are planting a budded rose, how deep you position the bud union depends on where you garden.** Northern, Midwestern (if you're exposed to cold winds), and high mountain gardeners should plant the bud union below soil level—the colder the winters, the deeper (to a 4-inch maximum depth). Temperate and warm climate gardeners should leave the bud union above ground. In Brooklyn, I plant with the bud unions at ground level.

Newly planted roses should be watered immediately and generously. Cornell University has been studying the benefits of using club soda to water newly planted roses. The claim is that the carbonation is beneficial to the newly developing root system. My initial watering consists of manure tea (see **May**), and I continue with this every two weeks as long as the weather remains cool.

Avoid chemical fertilizers at planting time. They'll burn the newly emerging feeder roots. Instead, using 100 percent organic fertilizers will enrich the soil, creating an ideal environment for root development. **Remember: Strong-growing roots translate to strong-growing plants.** Since roses tend to grow much faster on top than underground, anything you can do to increase the root development will only benefit the plant in the long run. Put the new roses onto your fertilizer program after they have had a flush of bloom (if they are ever-bloomers), or in midseason (once-bloomers).

There are special fertilizers often referred to as root stimulators, available from specialty garden centers, online, or mail-order catalogs. If you would like to experiment with these, follow the directions given on the package. Use them now, with your newly planted rose. I prefer to use manure tea and fish emulsion to help get my roses started.

If you've purchased **potted roses**, they are planted in the same way as a bare-root rose, but skip the root pruning part. Just pop the rose out of its pot and into a prepared hole, keeping as much of the soil attached as possible. "Tease" the roots to loosen them before backfilling the hole. This encourages the roots to break the mold of the container.

During one of the spring meetings of the Heritage Rose Foundation in Natchez, Mississippi, we were planting roses in a cemetery. I spied someone using a posthole digger. How odd, I thought (now that I look back on this meeting, how odd it must have seemed to see us *all* wandering through the cemetery with digging tools!).

"Well it makes a perfect hole—it's clean; you can bring your wheelbarrow right up to it; and it's a lot easier," was the reply to my inquiry challenging this technique. Hmm, I thought, easier? Maybe if you're digging in clay soil, more common throughout the Southeast. With my sandy loam soil, I prefer to use a spading fork, loosening up as much soil as possible when I dig. Whichever way you choose to plant a rose, here's an old saying worth remembering: "Never plant a five-dollar rose in a fifty-cent hole."

**Roses need room to grow.** If you crowd rosebushes in your garden they will become troublesome in a very short time. Be generous with their spacing—in general, the larger the mature plant, the farther apart. For example, in my zone 7 garden, hybrid teas should be given at least 2 feet, while shrub roses (including old garden roses) should be separated by at least 3 feet. Smaller plants such as miniature roses and many of the polyanthas shouldn't be planted more closely than 12 inches apart. Climbers and ramblers need plenty of space between them. Plant them at least 6 feet from each other.

Above-ground growth always can be kept in check by pruning. One of the problems with planting roses too closely is the root competition. Always remember that what you see above ground is matched by an even more intricate system of roots, reaching deep and far into the soil in search of water and nutrients. Allow room for this to happen.

**The growing space each rose occupies does vary greatly from climate to climate, and even locally from garden to garden.** I have yet to see a rose perform as the catalogs or picture books promise they will. Little diagrams with dimensions such as 2 feet by 3 feet given to describe the growth habit of a particular variety should be taken lightly. For example, our heat and humidity tends to make many shrub roses grow more vegetative growth than you expect. Aware of this, I usually double any dimension that I see in English publications when I order roses from England for the Cranford rose garden.

Allow roses more room to grow if you are gardening in a climate that has mild winters and a long growing season. Shrubby roses in the north can easily become climbers in the south. I recently visited New Orleans to do a pruning demonstration. In preparing for my talk, I asked what type of climbing roses were growing there. The response was that any rose planted in this subtropical climate can become a climber.

There can also be growth differences between the same cultivars when one plant is budded and the other is on its own roots. I experienced this with shrub rose 'Alchymist'. I've grown a budded version in Brooklyn for years where it maintains a growth habit of about three feet high and wide. An 'Alchymist' on its own root system planted in another garden (in the same climate) has reached nearly four feet wide and is reaching tall enough to train onto an archway, a distance of at least 15 feet, and all in two years' time.

**Lack of vigor can also be due to a poor bud union.** But, unfortunately, there is another possible explanation for the difference in vigor between these two plants. **Rose mosaic virus** is a debilitating disease that can, among other things, diminish the vigor of rose bushes. This is a serious problem among budded roses.

Not at all limited to just modern roses, the virus begins to rear its ugly head as new foliage begins to grow. Distorted growth and severely crinkled foliage are signs of possible virus contamination. Often virus goes undetected until the leaves start turning into beautiful variegated forms, or displaying blotches of yellow, crinkled edges, ring patterns (single rings or even concentric arrangements), or a mottling as subtle as different shades of green on a leaf. One of the problems with virus detection is that many of these symptoms can be discounted as something other than virus (black spot, mildew). If a rose is infected, it may not show any symptoms at first. Then suddenly you'll start noticing odd changes as the plant begins to enter its first flush of bloom. Virus can lay dormant, too. You might notice it today, but in a week's time, the symptoms will have disappeared as the virus retreats into dormancy until next year.

Rose mosaic virus is actually a complex of different viral diseases, found in both wild and cultivated roses. It was thought for the longest time that rose viruses did nothing to affect the flower production and vigor of a rosebush. Research in laboratories and in the field have prove this to be untrue. Besides decreasing vigor, a virus can make a plant more susceptible to winter damage; flower production can be diminished or the flowers themselves deformed; foliage and new growth can be discolored and deformed; and finally, bud grafts can fail as a result, meaning the top plant will die and the understock take over.

So far, there hasn't been any proof that virus can be spread in your garden from plant to plant, unless you do your own budding. An infected bud inserted into another rose plant (such as a root stock) will spread the virus. Pruning from an infected rose to a "clean" rose will not spread the virus.

Virus has been a sore spot among rosarians for a very long time, and will be for a while. At first, many nurseries refused to acknowledge its existence, or the effect it has on the growth of roses. Today, however, growers are taking steps to clean their stock of virus-infected plants. It's interesting to note that in *The Plant Disease Handbook* (Westcott, 1950), Dr. Westcott reported that rose mosaic virus was common on garden roses on the Pacific Coast and only in greenhouses in the East. Today, this is a problem of international concern.

The responsibility for correcting this problem lies with the rose nurseries that propagate and grow roses. Only they can do something to correct this problem. The growers need to rid their growing fields and greenhouses of virus-infected plants.

There are several virus-cleaning programs using extremely hot temperatures to kill the virus for the commercial trade—set up by at least two universities, Florida Southern College and the University of California at Davis. **These heat treatment programs will rid plants of virus.** In addition to this, the commercial growers should only use virus-free rootstocks and clean budding material when producing their roses that eventually end up in our gardens. There is nothing that the home gardener can do but to look out for the symptoms and raise a fuss with any nursery that sells you an infected plant. In my garden I ignore it among my older plants. Since I don't exhibit I'm not alarmed by the yellow patterns that show up occasionally on some of these roses. However, I do notice a distinctive lack of vigor in these plants. New arrivals that show a virus—that's a different story. Those nurseries hear from me the day the virus first appears.

April is quickly slipping away. **I still have a little bit of pruning to do.** Now that spring is here to stay, I prune Chinas, teas, Bourbons, and Noisettes.

## CHINA

This is a class of roses that has its roots way back in the ancient civilizations of China and other regions of the Far East. As Westerners, our experience with these roses dates from the 1790's when the first of these roses were brought to America with the English and French colonists.

Unlike any roses grown before, these new roses were everblooming (monthly) and, in the right climates, evergreen. From two early Chinese introductions, 'Old Blush' and 'Slater's Crimson China', a whole new class evolved due to the maddening hybridizing that occurred in England, France and the United States during the nineteenth century.

The new class that quickly evolved was composed of everblooming plants that were best suited to climates with mild winters. The original shrubby, twiggy varieties that won the hearts of many over two hundred years ago are still with us today (though often the subject and cause of many a mystery in the rose world) as well as many wonderful hybrids, perfect for warm weather and temperate gardens.

Twiggy is the key to the main growth habit of these roses. They can survive decades, maybe even centuries, of neglect, but always look best in the garden if they have an annual shaping and thinning out.

## TEA

Tea roses are not hybrid tea roses. A tea rose was involved with the creation of the first hybrid tea rose, but that's where the association ends. Furthermore, tea roses have nothing to do with tea, or at least nothing to do with the making of tea. The original tea roses were discovered, like the ancient China roses, in the Far East; first brought to England by the East India Tea Company. Stories of the origin of the name for this class are numerous, the two most popular being: The roses were transported out of China in tea crates or, when the crates containing these roses were first opened, the air was perfumed with an unmistakable fragrance of tea. Take your pick. They both make for interesting conversation at rosarian cocktail parties.

Regardless of the meaning of the class name, these roses seemed to be advanced China roses with a wider color palate. It's through this cold-sensitive group that the first apricot-colored roses were recorded (a beautiful rose named 'Safrano', still with us today). Together with the China roses, tea roses became the rage of the continent during the nineteenth century. In conservatories and gardens throughout nineteenth century America, gardeners fell in love with the long stems of nodding roses, borne on vigorous plants of twiggy and dense growth.

I have been warned by southern gardeners not to prune tea roses very much—they resent being pruned, is the claim. This may be true, but often I have no choice but to prune them very low, if not to the ground level, with simply the removal of deadwood resulting from winter kill. This makes pruning of these roses easy for me.

If you garden in the South, in California, or any temperate climate where these roses grow into huge shrubs, prune according to how you want them to fit into your garden design. Always remove dead and twiggy wood from the center. Tea roses are spectacular if they are allowed to grow into large, rounded shrubs. They can be very ugly if left alone for many seasons.

## NOISETTE

A true American native, the first rose of this class was created near Charleston, South Carolina, in the late 1700's. An offspring of a China rose and the musk rose (a cold-sensitive species), this American seedling was sent to the Noisette family nursery in France where their interest in it spawned an entirely new class bearing their family name.

Known for producing large clusters of flowers (usually soft pastel colors) and a vigorous growing habit, Noisettes are often the choice for climbers in temperate and warm climates, and as shrubs of various sizes in gardens with colder winters. There are only a few that can be used as short-growing climbers in my garden ('Mme. Alfred Carrière' and 'Princesse de Nassau'); the rest are medium to low growing shrub roses. A series of beautiful golden yellow-pink Noisette cultivars were created in the nineteenth century using yellow tea roses as a parent. Serious collectors refer to these as **Tea-Noisettes**. The Tea-Noisettes are some of the most beautiful and vigorous roses known ('Crépuscule', 'Jaune Desprez', and 'Gloire de Dijon,' to name a few). Rampant climbers throughout the warm areas of our country, these roses are not happy in zones with a serious winter.

Noisettes should be thinned annually of deadwood. As they age, remove some of the oldest wood, too. If they grow as shrubs in your garden, then prune them as you would an everblooming shrub rose. If they have a climbing habit in your climate, treat them the way you would any everblooming climbing rose.

## BOURBON

Among the hardiest of all of the China rose mixes, the Bourbon rose class has its origins on an island in the Indian Ocean, Réunion Island (formerly Île de Bourbon). Reportedly, on this island, there was a hedge of the China rose 'Old Blush' growing near a hedge of damask roses (allegedly 'Autumn Damask'). A new rose was found growing near the hedges, and it was assumed that this was an accidental seedling of the two hedge roses.

By 1819, the seedling had made its way to the gardens of King Louis Philippe (the last monarch of the Bourbon family), near Paris. The name

Bourbon, in reference to the island as well as a tribute to the king, became attached to future generations of this seedling.

Many of the Bourbons today are everblooming and can be grown as climbing roses in warmer climates. There are a few that are successful climbers in cold climates as well, but there are many more that are grown as shrubs in northern climates.

Bourbons benefit from a severe pruning, otherwise they tend to become too dense. This is a problem since they are prone to black spot. Any long canes should have their tips cut back, and any lateral growth off these long canes should be shortened to a few inches. Bourbon roses are excellent candidates for pegging; also for wrapping around pillars or other tall structures in the garden.

After my pruning and planting are finished, I spend the remainder of the month removing the remains of winter mulch from the plants, scattering the mulch into the rose beds. Now is the time to look for dieback on any pruning that was finished last month. In fact, there should be signs of life on all of the roses. If leaf buds haven't begun to grow after the first month since pruning, or if there is some death due to a late blast of cold weather, cut the canes again to the next healthy growing bud.

As April nears May, I have to remember to put the tea roses back into their pots. These are teas that I bury every winter, back in an out-of-the-way corner. During the season they grow in large containers, decorating the steps leading into the rose garden. In the autumn, when they've finished blooming, I heel them in again in their protected corner area for safekeeping. Now it's time to lift them out, clean them up (there's always deadwood to prune), and then repot them.

With all of the work going on and the mud being flung, don't forget to look around to see what is happening in the rose garden. If you are growing the species rose *Rosa rubiginosa* (also known as *R. eglanteria*, or the 'Eglantine Rose') or any of its hybrids, you can't help but notice them now. There should be an unmistakable fragrance of green apples, especially obvious during dewy mornings. This fragrance is coming from the newly emerging leaves.

The early tulips are beginning to bloom, as well as the small pink flowering bulb *Chionodoxa* 'Pink Giant'—a favorite of mine for scattering throughout the rose beds. When you underplant your garden with these delicate beauties, it does require a bit more care when you're planting and pruning. Watch for signs of other spring bulbs as well. My old garden roses are under planted with fragrant narcissus, every year there are more and more of them filling in around the new growth of the roses with pale yellow and white flowers. As May nears, the tulips will soon be putting on quite a show. Down along the Gulf Coast, the ancient red amaryllis some call 'St. Joseph's Lily' is blooming along with the first spring flush of tea and China roses.

You may notice that some species and old roses have a white speckle on some of the foliage. At close inspection you might not see any responsible insects, but a likely suspect is the **rose leafhopper.**

Found throughout the United States, the nymph stage of this European flying insect feeds on the leaf tissue of roses—mainly the species roses. Seeming to appear suddenly overnight, the eggs have been hidden through the winter in the canes of the roses they are feeding on. This first generation of this insect will feed on the rose leaves, mature quickly, and move on to other plants. They are especially fond of other plants in the rose family, not just roses. (See list at end of chapter.) I tend to find them in roses planted near crab apple trees (a member of the rose family). They'll spend successive generations that season among the leaves of the rose family relatives before returning to the rose canes for winter hibernation.

Leafhoppers don't cause a problem for me. I only have a small population, and I also suspect that they are the reason I have so many warblers in the garden during spring.

Leafhoppers can be controlled with the help of beneficial insects known as lacewings. As for chemical sprays, biodegradable insecticides containing pyrethrum and rotenone-based compounds are effective (see **August**). Sticky-tape traps that can be hung among the shrubs will also work to control their population. But is all of this trouble worth it? Probably not. The life cycle of leafhoppers in the rose garden is short, usually finished by the time the hybrid teas come into bloom. And, their damage is nothing more than a cosmetic problem. I'd recommend that you ignore them.

**All around me I see the beauty of the rose garden starting.** New foliage on all of the species and many of the ramblers give the garden a greenish glow. Now that the pruning and most of the planting is finished, I begin to feel anticipation for the new rose that is just around the corner.

Friends in Texas and South Carolina are already enjoying flushes of blooms from species and many of the old garden roses. This is also the month when many rose societies in California are celebrating their roses as they come into full bloom. One noteworthy collection in southern California is the Huntington Botanical Gardens in San Marino, California.

The everblooming roses I plant in April will bloom in June. The species and once-blooming old roses I planted may bloom the first year, but only a with a minimal display. These will be stunning next year. I can never believe it as I look at my newly planted, sticklike bushes in the ground. Getting your new roses in the ground and giving each plant the best growing conditions possible are the most important parts of the job. The work pays off. So find that perfect spot and start to loosen the soil. Work in some compost and manure. Wait. Loosen up a little more. And wait.

---

## RECOMMENDED READING

*Consulting Rosarians Manual.* American Rose Society. Compiled by the Consulting Rosarian Committee, Louise Coleman, Chairman. Shreveport, LA. Second edition 2001.
 —*Available from the American Rose Society*

## LIST OF COMMON GARDEN PLANTS IN THE ROSE FAMILY

**Trees**
 Cherry
 Apple
 Crab Apple
 Pear
 Peach
 Apricot

**Shrubs**
 Quince
 Flowering Almond
 Spirea
 Pyracantha

**Perennials**
 Strawberry
 Lady's Mantle

## SOME COMPANION BULBS TO CONSIDER

 St. Joseph's Lily *(Hippeastrum × johnsoni)*
 Poetica narcissus
 Jonquil narcissus
 Tazetta narcissus
 Triandrus narcissus
 *Chionodoxa*
 Kaufmanniana Tulips
 Turkestan Tulip

[1]Dr. Malcolm Manners, The Cherokee Rose. Lakeland, Fla.: Central Heritage Rose Society, 1993.

# MAY

The race is on for the first in bloom. Every spring for the last ten years, the first rose to come into bloom in Brooklyn is the species *Rosa carolina*, followed closely by the near-white, four-petaled species, *Rosa omeiensis* (the only rose known to have four petals). Our plant of this rare rose was grown from seed actually collected in China, near the Himalayan Mountains. More than the flower, I find the large, translucent red prickles on every emerging new cane to be absolutely beautiful and most interesting. The armed canes, backlit by the sun, create an impression of brilliant rubies in the garden.

Each day in May that I spend in the garden has something new to offer, as more and more of the species and old garden roses begin to show color. The eglantines are now freely emitting apple fragrances from their foliage. The 'Incense Rose' (*Rosa primula*) holds the title for the most unusual foliar fragrance, said to remind some, with exotic imaginations, of Russian leather. Let the spectacle begin!

"How much Epsom salt can be applied to roses to repel deer and control aphids?" This was an actual phone message I received one May from a television producer, one that I should've answered immediately. Instead, I let this person get away with the delusion and misinformation that Epsom salts are the cure-all for rose garden problems. And sure enough, a few days later on national television an infamous celebrity garden "know it all" was touting the deer-repellent qualities of this homemade spray.

Chemically speaking, **Epsom salts is a brand name for magnesium sulfate.** Horticulturally speaking, magnesium is one of the many naturally occurring elements (a trace element) that plants utilize to grow stronger and bloom better. For roses, adding magnesium encourages new growth from the base of the plant (from the bud union of grafted roses) and promotes a greener leaf. That's the *only* use I know of for Epsom salts in the rose garden. It does nothing to repel aphids or deer. (I'm sure they sold a great deal of Epsom salts that day!)

I use Epsom salts once a year after pruning. I scratch into the soil, around the base of my roses, approximately ¹/₄ cup. I also follow the advice of my friends from New Orleans and add, at the same time, ¹/₄ cup of green sand.

One final word on Epsom salts: Use it for an evening tub soak following those long days of pruning, planting, or after a long night of chasing deer!

There are all sorts of new organic fertilizers on the market to explore—some from sources you never would have imagined. One year I tried a new product composed of the droppings of crickets. Yes, I said crickets. (I didn't buy it; it was a gift from a friend.) Now let me tell you, I have a strong tolerance for natural fragrances, but this was definitely pushing it to the limit. If I ever wanted to be alone in the garden, or get a seat on a crowded subway at rush hour, I knew that a day with this insect "stuff" would do the trick.

Speaking of droppings, one year the botanic garden (long before my time) accepted a donation of elephant manure from the local zoo. I don't think this will ever happen again, since the flea infestation outlasted any benefits that the manure might have brought to the garden.

A liquid fertilizer that I have great faith in for producing healthy, green foliage and strong root growth is **manure tea**. I use it from planting time in the spring until the temperatures go up past the high eighties, and again in early autumn once the weather begins to cool. Manure tea is 100% organic and, like all organic fertilizers, it works best during cooler weather periods.

If I can round up some fresh stable manure (cow or horse manure—chicken manure is great, too—and as fresh as possible), this becomes my main ingredient for tea. Sometimes I'll use fish tea, made from fish emulsion (which is ever part of the fish we won't eat, blended into an enticing syrup). **These teas are especially fragrant—good for keeping rude visitors out of the garden!**

## MANURE TEA CONCENTRATE
- Fill a large garbage can (25 gallons) to ¹/₅ full with your choice of manure;
- Add water, filling the can to the top;
- Stir frequently; and
- Cover the garbage can to keep any curious critters from falling in **(and to keep your neighbors happy!)**

To use manure tea in the garden, simply fill a bucket half-full with the tea concentrate (make sure you stir up the solution before you dip into it).

Add enough water to fill the bucket nearly to the top and you have the perfect dilution of manure tea.

It's much simpler (but perhaps more fragrant) to make a fish emulsion tea. I have found a wonderful product that has recently hit the shelves of most nurseries and garden centers that I am now using instead of straight fish emulsion. It's a blend of fish emulsion and seaweed sold in a liquid (fragrant) concentrate. Products with fish and seaweed (kelp) are excellent supplements to your fertilizer program. They provide the roses with nitrogen as well as valuable trace elements. Trace elements are essentially vitamins for the rose, working with the main fertilizer ingredients—nitrogen, potassium, and phosphorous—to further strengthen the plants.

## FISH EMULSION TEA
- 1 tablespoon of fish emulsion, or fish/seaweed concentrate; mix with
- 1 gallon of water

Look around in our garden and you might notice that some of the roses you planted last month still haven't started to grow. Weekly applications of tea should push them into growing. Continue giving each plant a gallon of the mixture each week until they're showing signs of strong growth. **A healthy rose should be producing lots of green leaves during the spring.** You can do this for all of your rose bushes as a supplemental feeding, but I tend to concentrate on just those that are off to a slow start.

Go around and re-prune any wood that is not growing at this time, whether it's on newly planted or established roses. You can completely remove the cane or cut it to where you see signs of life. This is also the chance to catch up on any damage that might have occurred as the result of a late freeze.

When using either manure or fish tea, this is a growth stimulant. But, the key element to get the roses to grow is water. **Water is absolutely essential for success with roses, especially those newly planted.**

The culprit behind many problems in the rose garden is often an inadequate watering system. I remember one craze when I was a kid: the walking hose cart. It supposedly wandered on its own, giving your lawn and garden a complete watering. All you had to do was turn on the water, and off it went. Today's watering systems are like the hot rods of the baby boomer generation. The level of sophistication (and water waste) in pop-up nozzles, oscillating heads, computers, etc., seems to be more a measurement of one's status in the neighborhood than what's best for the garden.

Pay attention to *when* and *how* you water. Too much water can be as bad for roses as not enough water. Also, the *way* you water can be especially crucial to the health of your roses.

Unless the garden is very large, I prefer to water with an hand held hose, with a water wand held down at the base of the plant. Not only this chore yet another opportunity to see what is going on in the garden, I enjoy this task. I find myself going into a slightly altered state as I stand with hose in hand.

I have a client who was perplexed by the fact that his roses only lasted for a short time on the bush. Immediately, I suspected the new water system that had been "custom designed" for the rose garden by the local landscaper. On a hunch, I went out into the garden before sunrise. I could hear the system before I saw it, and knew what I suspected was true. Water was oscillating with a terrible force from several state-of-the-art sprinklers hidden underground by day, but actively pumping out water all night long. These were aimed in every direction, spraying into— and over—the roses. In addition to this, the neighbor's shrub border was well watered!

Roses love water, but there's absolutely no reason to water your garden every day. The only situation I can think of that may require daily watering is a potted rose garden on a windswept terrace during the hottest part of the summer. Otherwise, you're wasting water, breeding fungi, leaching your fertilizer, and very possibly drowning your roses.

More important than how often you water is how *deep* you're watering. The entire root system (up to 2 feet deep) needs water. If the water doesn't go deep into the soil, you'll end up with lots of tiny, fibrous roots creating an impenetrable mat at the soil surface.

**Soil composition has a great deal to do with how much you water your garden.** You should find out how well your soil retains water before investing in expensive computers to run your irrigation system. Remember the test that uses a coffee can (see **April**). It's still not too late to do this simple test. Clay soil has a greater water retention quality than a sandy soil mix. If you are gardening in clay soil, you should not follow the watering recommendations from someone in a sandy region.

Go out into the garden a day after you have watered and probe with a sharp spade or a heavy bar into the rose bed. Shove the tool eighteen to 24 inches deep. Is the soil wet at that depth? If so, you've given enough water; if not, increase the length of your watering time. Is there a serious layer of muck under the rose? If so, you have too much water. For a sandy-loam mix with excellent drainage, an average of about one inch of water a week is sufficient. Clay soil will be significantly less.

When considering how to irrigate, you should also be thinking about mulch. The primary function of a mulch is to keep the plants from drying out, conserving water in the garden.

**Mulch is any material that is spread on the surface of the soil around the plants as a protective, as well decorative, element in the garden.** Mulch is absolutely essential for the rose garden. There's an old saying to the effect that roses like cool feet and hot heads. A good mulch layer will keep the roots cool and moist, producing a plant with the healthiest growth and most beautiful flowers.

Cooling the soil around the roots is another important benefit of using mulch. If you live in a particularly hot area of the country, go out into the garden during the hottest time of the day. You'll be amazed at how hot the surface of the soil is—almost too hot to touch. I discovered this in Dallas when the temperature had been hovering near 100 degrees Fahrenheit for nearly a week.

This heat will not promote growth. There are roots immediately beneath the soil, and when they get too hot or dry the roses go into a dormant state, especially when temperatures around the roots remain very high for any length of time. A thick layer of mulch will help to insulate the roots from the heat and lessen the speed of evaporation of water.

A third reason for using mulch: It will deter the growth of weeds. And who likes to weed in the heat? That's a good enough reason for me to start using a mulch.

The best time to apply mulch is also the most convenient time, when you've just finished pruning and planting, and at least one application of fertilizer has been put down. (For me this is early May). Water the beds first, or spread mulch during a light rain. This guarantees a well-moistened soil for the remainder of the spring growing season.

A final reason—and I hope that this will convince you to use mulch—is disease control. Putting down a layer of mulch can prevent over-wintered fungi spores on the ground from splashing up onto the canes of your roses.

Spread the mulch around the roses 2 to 3 inches thick. Come right up to the rose plants and out to the very edge of the beds.

As the mulch ages, periodically "fluff" it to keep it looking good and keep it loose for better movement of water and fertilizer to the soil and roots below. If you ever doubted the water conservation quality of mulch, you will discover through "fluffing" that there is plenty of moisture just beneath the mulch surface, even though the mulch itself might appear to be dry.

What kind of mulch should you use? There are many materials to choose from. Some definitely recommend themselves over others. A good mulch is one that eventually decomposes (but not too fast), increasing the organic content of the soil. Avoid mulches that do not "give back" to the garden in this fashion, such as black plastic, stone, and landscape cloth.

**Some of the best mulch materials to use are free—often throwaway materials from farms, breweries, or Mother Nature.** In order of most fragrant to not so fragrant, they are: manure (aged cow, two-week-old horse), beer hops, eelgrass (the stringy sea grass that covers many East Coast beaches), compost, shredded corncobs, pine needles, and shredded leaves.

I recommend aged over fresh cow manure for a good reason. Aged manure has "cooked" any weed seeds that passed through the animal. I used fresh cow manure once (it was sold to us as aged, but even a city slicker like myself could smell a discrepancy): I was pulling corn plants out of the garden well into July.

A favorite mulch for some gardeners (including me) along the coastal regions of the Northeast is eelgrass. Each tide washes up a fresh crop of the thin crinkly blades of near-black grass. Collect from the older piles and throw it right into your beds (if you take the oldest and driest, there isn't enough salt to do any damage). At first it might look as though the tide washed through your garden. But in a year's time, you'll have a beautiful new layer of coarse soil around your roses. I have improved my mom's sandy soil to a rich sandy loam through annual applications of eelgrass. What about the smell? It dissipates quickly, and it's nowhere as odiferous as manure. Nutrient-rich critters, such as dead crabs, seashells, and sometimes even dead fish, are an added bonus.

There are many packaged mulches that are beautiful to look at, in addition to being good for the soil. I'm very partial to shredded bark—cedar, pine, and hardwood are the most popular. Shredded licorice root, if you can stand the overpowering, not-at-all-like-licorice fragrance, is also very nice to look at. **I personally think that the dyed mulches (red, black, and brown) are hideous. Stick with the natural mulches!**

Some rosarians claim that pine chips act as a natural fungicide. They've based this observation on a notable decrease in the occurrence of black spot and mildew when using pine chips as a mulch. This is definitely worth looking into. Supposedly it's the smaller chips, rather than the large nuggets. That's good news. I think the smaller ones look nicer among roses, anyway.

Crushed stone is often used as a mulch, but I'd be concerned that the reflective heat from the stone mulch would invite spider mites to the garden (see **July**).

Some rosarians cultivate the soil instead of mulching. In fact, when I first took over the Cranford Rose Garden, I cultivated the soil, breaking it up around the plants with a long-handled claw tool. I enjoyed the exercise, and there is something about the moving of soil that I found very calming.

Even though no material has been added to the garden, this is still mulching. Every time the soil is cultivated, a dust layer of loose soil is formed. This is mulch. Frequent cultivation of the soil can be a hazard to the plants, however. Delicate feeder root near the surface can be broken during this process. And I have to admit that during hot and humid August days, I found I would rather be cultivating cool thoughts under a sprinkler than out in the hot sun pushing soil! After a couple of hot summers, it was only a matter of time before I started adding shredded cedar bark to the garden as a mulch.

Some mulches can induce the formation of hardpan. This will work against the plants, restricting water and air movement around the roots. I've experienced this problem with buckwheat hulls as a mulch. Attractive as they are, the small, flaky hulls are not easily decomposed. After several years of using this mulch in the garden, the soil developed into a hardpan.

When you use a mulch, don't forget that there is soil beneath the mulch. Ideally, it would be good to turn the mulch layer into the soil on an annual basis. The best time to do this would be in early spring after all of the planting is done. But if your soil is still fairly loose and the mulch is still intact, just freshen it up and wait another year before turning it in.

Older gardeners have a thing for peat moss as mulch. My grandfather would send me and my brothers into the woods to fill wheelbarrows with decayed logs—his favorite mulch (there were six of us—that was a lot of mulch!). If he couldn't get the rotted logs, then he would use peat moss. The problem with peat moss as a mulch is that it can repel water when it dries, and it may also absorb moisture from the soil. Both situations would not be good for the roses. So, I don't recommend peat moss as a mulch. But, if you have access to rotten logs, that's a great mulch.

Keeping good mulch will also lower your water bill. Keep this in mind when deciding what type of water system you are going to install. The most practical system to use (and most efficient) is one that keeps the foliage of the roses as dry as possible and gives enough water for thorough penetration. Leaky hoses, drip systems, emitter systems, and bubbler systems are all examples of this type. The water is kept at soil level. There is no splashing of water onto the foliage. This brings us to the golden rule of rose growing: **Never water your roses at night.**

If there is excessive moisture on the plant or on the surface of the soil in the evening, this is an open door to all sorts of problems. Fungi-related problems run rampant in this situation. Depending on the temperature of the air, you can expect to begin battle with the dreaded fungi-caused diseases: **black spot, powdery mildew, and downy mildew.**

Long, cool, moist springs are a dream come true for gardeners. However, humidity of 85 percent or higher and temperatures ranging from 65 to 80 degrees Fahrenheit are also ideal for the germination and spread of downy mildew, a disease currently taking many outdoor rose gardeners by surprise. Known for a long time as a greenhouse problem (where it's easily dealt with by raising temperatures and lowering humidity), downy mildew is more than unsightly—it's destructive.

Downy mildew occurs initially on the undersides of newer foliage. Often undetected, this disease can defoliate an entire bush, and can do it fast. Before the leaves fall off, you might notice purplish-red to dark brown spots on the leaves and canes. If you have this sudden drop, inspect the fallen leaves with a hand lens. It's sometimes possible to see the downy-like mildew that gives this disease its name on the underside of the foliage.

No one is really sure how this disease has entered our rose gardens, although it was initially recorded as a California disease. Nor are we sure of an ecologically safe way to treat it. Fungicides containing copper compounds will help to control this disease and some rosarians are experimenting with neem oil, a much safer alternative (for more on neem, see **August**).

The fungus that causes downy mildew can be spread either through shared cuttings or from plant to plant. No rose seems to be immune, but some rose varieties are more susceptible than others. I've seen it on the oldest gallicas as well as the newest hybrid tea roses. Whenever you buy a new plant, inspect it carefully for any of the symptoms. Gardens near the seaside or on the shores of large bodies of water are ideal settings for this disease. Downy mildew will not develop in hot or arid climates.

The fungus that causes downy mildew can over-winter in the garden in all parts of your rosebush and in garden debris, becoming active when conditions become favorable. **The best way to treat this disease is through prevention.** Keep your garden clean of all decay and remove any infected parts as soon as you suspect there might be a problem.

One retired rosarian from Pennsylvania once told me of his theory of washing off the roses every morning after an evening of high humidity. He claimed that you could actually wash off the spores that cause fungal problems. At the time, I thought he was crazy. Why would you want to get the leaves wet, I thought to myself? But current research on controlling fungal diseases has proven him right, especially with downy mildew. Researchers have had success with daily showers of warm water (over 80 degrees Fahrenheit) in experiments on ridding their roses of this dreaded disease.

By the middle of May, I have pretty strong evidence that there is going to be a rose display after all. The old garden roses are beginning to bloom, sort of an overture to the season. The gorgeous yellow blooms of 'Harison's Yellow' are cascading over the magenta hybrid rugosa 'Mme. Charles Frederic Worth'. Rose fever has definitely kicked in, as my rose garden volunteers and I begin keeping records of what's in bloom.

I'm also making notes on where I can plant more roses. With all of my bare-root roses safely in the ground and growing, I can still use a few more. It's the perfect time to raid the local garden centers in search of potted roses.

Who can resist the temptation of a potted rose in full bloom? Shop around and you will find roses for sale in just about every possible scenario: the fruit and vegetable stands, the local florist, hardware stores, at the farmers market, in the supermarket, discount department stores, large box stores, and of course at local garden centers. Forced into earlier-than-usual bloom, they give a preview of what to expect in your own garden.

Be a wise consumer: Don't be seduced by the pretty flowers. You want the best quality of plant possible, so look **beyond the flowers and carefully inspect the plants.** First of all, are they under knowledgeable care, or just stuck on the shelf for a quick sale? I don't buy roses that are on display indoors, and if I can't find someone who doesn't at least know the difference between a hybrid tea and a climber, forget it. The rose you want for your garden should be growing in as ideal a situation as possible and maintained immaculately by a knowledgeable staff. Don't bring the seller's problems home to your garden.

There should be a sturdy plant supporting the flowers. I usually buy the roses that aren't too advanced in bloom, but instead showing lots of emerging leaves with a rich green color. Search for a rosebush that has at least three strong canes. Four would be even better. I scan the crop for the healthiest-looking foliage. Shiny leaves are a promise of higher disease resistance. I avoid plants showing any signs of foliage spots or yellowing; stunted growth never makes it into my garden; and plants with split or blackened canes can go right to the compost pile as far as I'm concerned.

Packaging is a significant factor in my decision-making. If I can't stick my fingers into the potting mix, I go elsewhere. I want to see and feel what this rose has been growing in. I want a rose that looks as though someone was genuinely interested in its well-being. I prefer roses that are actually potted up at the nursery that is selling them. Poke around the pot to find out how the root systems are growing. I'm not crazy about roses in "ready to plant" boxes, or those sold in plastic bags with a colorful photo stapled to them. However, sometimes you will find some wonderful older hybrids in these packages. If you can't resist, make sure you give them a bit more TLC when you get home. I do not buy any roses that have waxed canes.

If the rosebush is in bloom, or coming into bloom, does the plant have a balanced appearance? With a blooming rose, I want one that is showing more than one flower or the promise of more than one. Lots of new flower buds and a healthy display of foliage is a sign that the rose is well cared for.

Most containerized roses in the local nursery are budded roses, and the bud union is usually easy to spot. Are they growing on the right rootstocks for your region (see **January**)? This is a pertinent question, for gardeners in Florida or anywhere else where nematodes could be a problem (see **September**). If you are buying a budded rose where soil nematodes are an issue, only buy those budded onto 'Fortuniana' rootstock.

A potted rose doesn't have to be planted with the urgency of a bare-rooted rose. One of the luxuries of this style is that you can leave it in the pot for a long time.

Then again, it's very easy to plant a potted rose: The garden should be prepared in the same fashion as for bare-root roses, then just make the hole slightly bigger than the pot.

## PLANTING A POTTED ROSE
To plant a potted rose, follow these steps:
A. If your potted rose is a budded rose, it is likely that the bud union will be position high
B. Dig a hole big enough to fit the pot. Pop the plant out of the pot without disturbing the roots. Position the plant on top of a compost layer so that the bud union is at the proper level for your region.
C. Water the newly planted rose thoroughly
D. You might want to create a catch basin by building up a ring of soil about a foot in diameter around the newly planted rose.

If you are having trouble getting the rose out of the pot, try this method. First, cut off the bottom of the pot. Next, place it in the hole. Make sure that if you have a budded rose, the bud union is at the proper level for your region (see **April**). Budded roses in pots are often potted with the bud union three to 4 inches above the soil level. Once you've positioned the rose at the right level, remove the pot by slicing down the sides of the pot and pulling it away from the roots, while the new plant is in the hole.

I begin foliar feeding in May, since all of the roses are now producing new leaves. Following the directions on the package, spraying the leaves

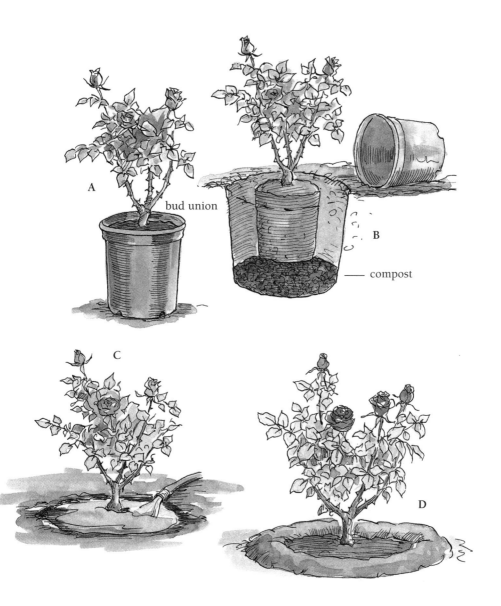

A *If your potted rose is a budded rose, it is likely that the bud union will be positioned high.*

B *Dig a hole big enough to fit the pot. Pop the plant out of the pot without disturbing the roots. Position the plant on top of a compost layer so that the bud union is at the proper level for your region.*

C *Water the newly planted rose thoroughly.*

D *You might want to create a catch basin by building up a ring of soil about a foot in diameter around the newly planted rose.*

with a water-soluble fertilizer is like giving the roses a shot in the arm. The frequency that you apply a foliar fertilizer varies among the different fertilizers. Basically, any houseplant fertilizer will do the job, sprayed twice a month. I especially like some of the new water-soluble *organic* fertilizers with their fishy smell, reminiscent of a tidal estuary in Brooklyn, sprayed once a month. One enormous benefit of the smelly fertilizer is that it keeps my visitors from stepping into the rose beds.

Recently, there has been some serious research using water soluble organic fertilizers as possible preventative cures for fungal diseases. Rosarians in Texas have noted a decline in the incidence of fungal diseases with frequent applications of these fertilizers as a foliar spray. For more on this, contact the **Houston Rose Society**.

Don't add more fertilizer thinking that you're going to get more roses. Not true! What you will create is great dining for aphids. During long, cool, spring days, they're already busy at work sucking sap from your bushes. Don't encourage them to get too comfortable.

**The cooler weather of spring is prime time for aphids.** Also known as plant lice or greenflies (though not always green), these soft-bodied sucking insects are easy to see. They're usually found clinging to every inch of the newest stems and coating unopened flower buds—sometimes several layers thick. Aphids are a threat to the well-being of your roses, often causing deformed growth and causing new growth and flower buds to wilt.

In warmer climates, aphids are continually active in the adult stage year round. In cold climates, aphids overwinter in the egg stage. The eggs are deposited among plant material and debris in the garden, in the autumn. Aphid eggs can also be carried by ants (who enjoy the sugary sap that the mature aphids exude) to their underground colonies for safe storage. It's possible that horticultural oils sprayed during the winter and early spring can destroy the eggs, but it doesn't take more than a small nest of eggs to explode into an infestation. Be aware, too, that you can bring aphids (and other unwanted guests) into your garden when you bring new plants from outside sources.

There are recommended insecticides of various levels of toxicity you can use to get rid of aphids. However, many safe alternatives are available, including dishwater, insecticidal soaps, lightweight horticultural oils, neem oil, and even a simple blast of water. Meanwhile, crushing a hundred or so with your bare fingers might relieve some frustration, but it's not really an effective pest management program (see **August** for more on alternative insecticide sprays).

There are many natural predators of aphids. Encourage them to multiply in your garden. One thing that I noticed when I stopped using insecticides, and started putting up birdhouses, was an increase in birds feeding on aphids in the rose gardens.

I have a new resident in my rose garden, the Eastern Bluebird, feeding all day on many insects. Even though they are predominately seed eaters, they definitely have been enjoying the delicacy of insects—especially aphids. I also have an abundance of warblers and kinglets stopping on their northward migratory paths during the month of May, hovering around the fresh new growth of the rosebushes.

The prettiest insect predator of aphids is the lady beetle—also known as the ladybug. There are many different types of ladybugs all over the country preying upon the adult aphids and their eggs. Their diet is not restricted to aphids, but includes mealybugs, scale, and even spider mites. The beetles feed during both their adult and larval stages. Every spring, I release new colonies of lady bugs into my garden (at night, so they don't fly away). You can purchase these online or in many garden centers.

**Aphid lions** are not lions at all, but instead the larva of the delicate lacewing flies. These voracious, at times, cannibalistic, creatures are a menace to the aphid population. They can devour hundreds of aphids before they are transformed into their adult form, the beautiful lacewing fly.

*Aphids are usually found clustering behind the flower. A strong jet of water will knock them off.*

Another fly that is a menace to the aphid population is the syrphid fly, also known as the flower fly or sweat fly. Resembling more a little bee or wasp, these miniature, brightly colored flies are usually seen hovering over the roses in search of nectar. The larvae, rather slug-like creatures, are a threat to the aphid population. The larvae have been observed destroying aphids at the rate of one per minute.

Aphids can also be destroyed by a very small parasitic wasp *Aphelinus abdominalis*. This wasp actually lays its eggs into the aphid. As the egg hatches and the larvae develop inside the aphid, the aphid dies.

Many beneficial insects are often already in the garden undetected. If you're not an aggressive insecticide user, they will remain in your garden and flourish. You can also purchase some from mail-order sources. The easiest way to increase the population of beneficial insects in your garden is to include companion plants with your roses that attract these friends. Many herbs and annuals that produce an umbel type of flower (basically a flat top, sort of umbrella-shaped bloom) such as yarrow, bronze fennel, and valerian are good attractants as well as beautiful to look at.

I also use many different members of the allium family (onion family) as companion plants. They seem to have a beneficial effect by controlling the population of bad and good insects in the garden. Many of these bulbs are now beginning to come into flower, and will remain in bloom as the roses come into their first flush. My favorite of the alliums is *Allium bulgaricum*, also sold as *Nectaroscordum siculum*, a 30-inch-tall perennial bearing clusters of pendulous cream-colored flowers. A perfect match for any rose color. The bulbs are small enough that they can be planted (in the autumn) right up against the rose bush. Plant them in clusters for the best display. Late summer brings on the blooms of another allium, *Allium tuberosome*, commonly known as garlic chives. These white flowers, on short stems, are a delight to see naturalizing through the old garden roses.

May is also the time for the peak of tulips that were planted last autumn. I use all types, from the earliest blooming hybrids to the tallest cottage forms. One fun combination is planting a mix of 'Queen of the Night' (dark purple) and 'Shirley' (white streaked with purple) under my *Rosa glauca*, the species rose with silver-pink foliage.

Working among the roses allows for many occasions to get a close inspection of the rosebushes and, especially, to look for pests such as aphids. One such opportunity is while edging the rose beds, a job I really enjoy doing. I string a line of twine, very taut, from one point to another along the proposed edge of the bed. With a tool known as a half-moon edger, I give the beds a nice, clean, straight edge. The edger works with foot power only. By pushing my entire weight onto a well-sharpened edger with a rocking motion, I cut through the lawn. As I pull up the cut grass, all kinds of treasures are unearthed—good and bad. Sometimes, I come across a toad or a turtle hatchling—these are welcome guests (hopefully, an entire toad or turtle, but then half of these critters make a good organic additive to the soil!). There are many earthworms, which I throw into the beds. If the birds don't get them first, they're great for the soil. Robins and catbirds follow me closely, hoping for the occasional handout, which usually consists of worms accidentally cut in half by the edger, or better yet, the uninvited guests that I search for this time of year—grubs.

Grubs are the larvae of flying beetles, and there are many different kinds. Most common and most devastating are the grubs of Japanese beetles. As grubs, they're harmless to the roses, but it won't be long before they mature. They're on their way up from deep hibernation. In a few weeks they'll mature into the dreaded beetle, that is, if they can escape the wrath of my fingers.

Squash them, throw them off of tall buildings (penthouse dwellers), or feed them to the birds, but don't let them stay in your garden. I knew a jealous gardener who threw them into a neighbor's rose beds. That's not a wise move, since the adult beetle will no doubt find its way back to your garden after feasting on the neighbor's!

Getting rid of the Japanese beetle larvae is the first line of defense for dealing with the less vulnerable, but more elusive, adult form (see **June** for dealing with the adults). Fortunately, there are some very safe and effective biological controls. To get the best results, you need to treat the lawn areas, where they hide, not the rose beds.

The most popular is Milky Spore Disease, available through many mail-order sources. This is a bacteria that attacks the grubs as they are on their way to the surface. Applying it year after year makes the bacteria stronger and more effective in controlling your grub population.

Diatomaceous earth (again, from mail-order sources or maybe in your local garden center) applied to the lawns will also knock off an emerging grub or two.

Studies have shown that neem oil used as a soil soak prevents young Japanese beetle larvae from developing into adults. This route is definitely worth pursuing (see **August** for more on neem oil).

There are faster-acting, highly toxic chemicals available. Anything that's labeled for grub control (usually in the lawn care section of a nursery) will cure your garden of this problem, but I often wonder what long term effects this type of chemical has on the water table and the health of the gardener. Where does it all eventually end up? And I've noticed with these granular types of pesticides that birds can't tell the difference between seeds and the chemical until it's too late.

And what about deer? Deer love roses, especially as the plants are just getting ready to bloom. My mom, who lives near woods that are over-crowded with deer, rarely got to see her roses in bloom until she discovered the powers of garlic. She has had good luck with garlic powder (*not* garlic salt!). Mom buys huge containers of the store-brand stuff and sprinkles it around the garden every night. Guess what—deer are less than adventuresome epicures. Since she started this routine, mom's roses are actually setting buds this season, and if everything goes right, we'll see some roses next month.

Back in Brooklyn, as I stand in the garden at the end of May, I begin to anticipate the arrival of summer. Everywhere I look I see color—not blocks of color, but enough to give me confidence that there will be a wonderful display after all. Visually, the sharp edge of the beds and the mulch make a big difference. The manicured, green lawns surrounding each bed add a lushness to the display. All I need now is a few warm, sunny days. With June just around the corner, I can finally begin to smell the roses.

---

## RECOMMENDED READING AND MEMBERSHIP
Regarding organic sources and control of insects and diseases:
*The IPM Practioner: Directory of Least Toxic Pest Control Products.* Bio-Integral
   Resource Center. Berkeley, CA.

Bio-Integral Resource Center
   PO Box 7414
   Berkeley, CA 94707
   510-524-2567
   **www.birc.org**
   Membership available: various levels

## PLANTS TO USE TO ATTRACT BENEFICIAL INSECTS AND WASPS
   Bronze Fennel
   Yarrow
   Heliotrope
   *Valerian officinalis* (Garden Heliotrope)
   Society Garlic
   Many members of the allium family, especially:
      *Allium bulgaricum* (*Nectaroscordum siculum*)
      Garlic Chives

# JUNE

I can smell them before I see them, the June roses, now in glorious bloom. Returning from the long Memorial Day weekend, which for me marks the beginning of the rose season, I approach a garden exuding fragrance and overflowing with roses. The same garden, only days ago, was decorated with just a smattering of color; this phenomenal change was wrought by the briefest spell of very warm weather.

The list of what's in bloom has grown in a mere month's time from a dozen or so to hundreds of varieties. Every rose class is on display, from the ancient species to the newest landscape shrub rose. It's time to rediscover old favorites or to get acquainted with the loveliest ingénues added to the garden this spring. Many of those planted only in April will bloom now, while once-blooming old roses planted *last* spring and fall will begin showing their stuff for the first time this season. **There are roses in bloom now**, such as the damasks and albas that have unforgettable fragrances and unusual colors. If you don't stop to enjoy them, they'll soon be gone—gone, that is, until next June.

Nothing is more satisfying than bringing in a fresh-cut bouquet of roses from the garden, especially when by doing so you're strengthening your rosebushes. Cutting is also a form of pruning, and pruning, as I said earlier, promotes more healthy growth. Besides, why are you growing roses if you're not going to cut at least some of them for the house? But a word of warning: Once the word is out that your garden's in bloom, you'll find your social calendar suddenly very full—it happens to me every year! Go. Get out there and cut some flowers. You've been real good to your roses; now go enjoy them. It's payback time.

I find the best time to cut a rose is in the morning, before the sun has had a chance to rob the flower of its fragrant oils. I look for flowers that

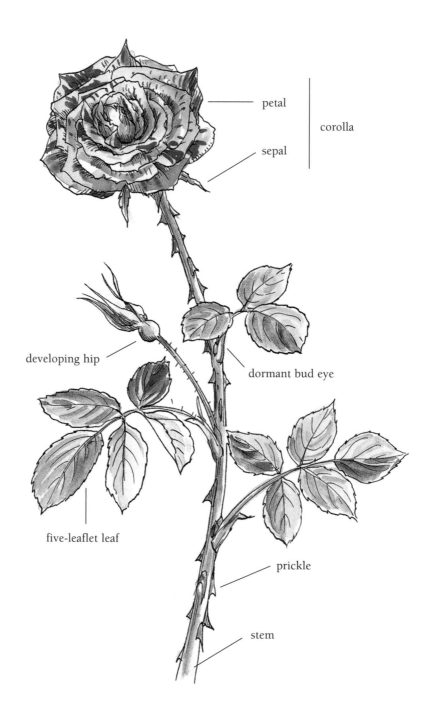

petal

corolla

sepal

developing hip

dormant bud eye

five-leaflet leaf

prickle

stem

*The anatomy of a rose.*

are fully opened, as well as those with closed, but not too tight, buds. When I say not too tight, it means that I can actually see several rows of petals starting to unfurl when I look straight into the nose of the flower.

Have a bucket of water with you to keep the roses as fresh as possible. Re-cut the stems with the stems submerged *in* the water, immediately after taking them from the bush. By re-cutting the flowers in this fashion, the intake of air into the stem is prevented. Air in the flower stem will cause a blockage, preventing water from being absorbed to keep the cut roses fresh. Once in a vase, the stem of a cut rose will eventually callus again preventing the uptake of water to the flower. To insure the longest possible life for your blooms, give each stem a new cut every day—always under water. This, and fresh, room temperature water in the vase, are all you need to make your garden roses outlast any store-bought rose.

It's simple to cut a rose, but it's not mindless. You should cut the blooms off the bush in the same manner that you would prune a faded flower. The removal of faded blossoms is referred to as deadheading. Now is the time to start deadheading; this, too, strengthens rosebushes.

Before you start chopping (whether you're cutting fresh or faded blooms), it is helpful to know a little bit about botany, with a focus on the leaf and stem of a rose.

A rose plant has compound leaves. A compound leaf is a leaf composed of a number of smaller leaves, of leaflets, joined together by a common branch known as a petiole. The compound leaves of roses are usually composed of three, five, seven (and so on) leaflets. Some of the species roses, such as *Rosa spinosissima*, have as many as fifteen leaflets.

The point where the petiole joins the main stem is the location of a bud, or growing point. This little green bump will eventually grow and produce a flower. Buds are located in a spiral pattern down the entire length of every rose branch, and always where a petiole joins the branch. The farther down they are from the tip of the branch, the more viable the buds become.

**With many roses—especially among hybrid teas—the best flower producing, growth will come from a bud that is located where there are leaves composed of five leaflets or more.** For this reason, I always try to cut to a bud where I count five leaflets. This is an excellent rule to follow, providing the rose you are deadheading *has* leaves composed of five leaflets.

The buds need to be stimulated to break dormancy and begin to grow. This is what happens when you cut a cane, or when a cane is broken, or even as a flower fades. The buds closest to the break or faded

*Whether you're cutting a rose for the house or removing a faded bloom, it's always best if you can cut the stem above the first set of five leaflets (A). New blooms will emerge from the dormant buds located where these leaves join the stem (B).*

flower will grow first. If the rosebush is an ever-blooming rose, and the small buds nearest the faded flower are allowed to grow, you'll end up with a much smaller bloom on the subsequent flower. The actual task of deadheading can vary from the removal of a single bloom, to pinching individual spent blooms from a cluster, to removing a good portion of the rosebush by removing long lengths of flowering branches for fresh-cut long-stemmed roses.

If you can't find a leaf of five leaflets, then just cut above any outward facing leaf. The dormant buds always grow in the direction that the leaf below the cut is pointing. Keep in mind that whenever you cut a rosebush, especially when deadheading or taking roses for the house, this is pruning. And whenever you prune a rosebush, you want to direct the new growth in an outward direction.

With clustered flowered roses, simply keep pinching the faded blooms from the cluster. Once the entire cluster is finished, cut the stem at a strong bud below the cluster. It's very possible that you won't find a leaf below the cluster. In this case, cut the stem bearing the faded cluster so that the remaining stem isn't sticking out like a sore thumb.

'Mlle. Cécile Brunner' and many other polyantha roses produce huge sprays of tiny roses from midsummer right through to frost. The sprays can become very complicated, sometimes composed of clusters within clusters with no visible signs of dormant buds. And many of the China or tea roses don't seem to have any dormant buds on their smooth canes. Where should you cut?

Watch what happens after a deer or rabbit chews back the tips of your roses, or when you accidentally slice a prize miniature rose with a weed whacker or a lawn mower. In a couple of weeks, lots of new green shoots will start growing from various points below the broken cane and from the base of the plant. Even though you couldn't see the buds, they were there.

Deadheading prevents a rosebush from developing hips. When an everblooming rose starts to create a hip, its re-blooming potential may be diminished. For this reason, concentrate on deadheading the ever-blooming roses and let the once-bloomers start to form hips.

Nothing looks worse than a faded bloom of an old garden rose or a hybrid tea rotting and turning to brown mush while still on the plant. One variety that is notorious for looking bad immediately after blooming in my humid climate is the white hybrid rugosa 'Blanc Double de Coubert'. Meaning no disrespect to Monsieur Coubert, after a day in our humidity, this rose resembles a double-sized dirty handkerchief. Grow this rose, and you'll quickly understand the value of deadheading.

*Sometimes with clustered flowered roses one bloom fades before the rest of the cluster is finished. In that case just pinch off the ugly center bloom.*

There are a couple of reasons why a rose's petals could turn prematurely brown. One is a disease known as **botrytis blight**. Botrytis is especially prevalent when flowers are frequently wet, the air is warm, and the humidity is high. At first the petals will merely appear to be bruised, but they will soon turn to mush. Other times, the flowers simply fail to open, or result in a shattered mess of brown petals. This is very common with very densely petaled roses; one in particular is the charming (but messy) pale pink polyantha 'Clotilde Soupert'. This disease is not selective among the different rose classes. It can happen to any rose with many petals. The best thing for preventing botrytis is to **eliminate any over-head watering and** deadhead any infected flowers immediately to prevent the fungus from spreading.

Another reason for browning of rose petals is the tiny insect known as a **thrip**, which is easy to spot while you're deadheading your roses. Thrips are new pests for me, but common to anyone who grows roses in a warm climate or greenhouse. The thrip that does the most damage in the rose garden is often referred to simply as the flower thrip. Barely visible to the naked eye, these flying insects scrape the delicate surface of the rose petals with their jaws—the injury resulting in unsightly brown streaks.

The damage is done by adult thrips as well as by the larvae deep inside the bloom. Their preference for light-colored roses makes them a real nuisance in the garden; otherwise they might not be as noticeable. However,

*Botrytis blight turns rose petals into mush*

when the infestation is severe, they can also cause a tightly wrapped rose to shatter when you touch it.

If you have a problem with thrips, it's imperative that you keep your garden free of fallen petals and rose leaves. Before the new larvae become full-fledged adults, they live a short period on the ground, usually in the garden litter of decaying foliage and fallen petals. Deadheading must be kept up with regularly. But do not compost these old flowers. Throw them away.

Thrips don't spend their whole life among the roses. They'll move to other parts of the garden, often overwintering in weeds (especially in dandelions and members of the nightshade family), grasses, citrus trees, onion fields, and shade trees. This should be kept in mind when trying to control their population.

For thrips, as for all insects, there are various chemicals available to control them. Whatever you use has to get inside the bloom and soak the soil. **Recent studies have shown that repeated applications of neem oil will control the infestation of thrips by killing them before they mature.** There has reportedly been some success using pyrethrum-based sprays as well. But if you can stand the smell, some gardeners claim that a garlic juice sprayed on the rose will act as a thrip repellent.

Diatomaceous earth spread around the rose plant is effective in controlling the ground-borne larval stage, and yellow sticky tape traps also work to control the thrip population. Recent studies have shown that applications of Wilt-Pruf (an anti-transpirant) have been successful in controlling the thrip population in greenhouses. Another thrip, the red-banded thrip, is a nuisance in Florida gardens in November. For more on this creature, see **November**.

To many of us, roses in June mean one thing for sure: **Japanese beetle**. They don't really come in overnight, even though it may seem that way. The larvae (grubs) were rearing their ugly heads in May. If you missed them then, you sure won't miss them now.

There is little so disgusting as finding 'Queen Elizabeth' covered entirely with these colorful iridescent chewing insects. Mounds of them can engulf one rose, feeding *and* copulating in the middle of the day! They're fast workers. Not only can they eat their way through entire gardens—leaves, flowers, and all—in a very short time, but in her forty-five days as an adult, the female can lay up to sixty eggs. The newly hatched larvae return to the soil and hibernate under your lawns until the following summer.

They've traveled far and wide since their accidental introduction into the United States. They allegedly arrived into the states in 1916, by way of

*Japanese beetles will eat all parts of any rosebush.*

a flight, from the Far East, into a Trenton, New Jersey airport. Today, their southernmost limit is northern Georgia, near Atlanta, their range extending west to California, as far north as Nova Scotia.

There appears to be no regular pattern to the dining habits of the beetles, except that they prefer a sunny situation for feasting. If you're growing pale-colored roses, or very fragrant roses, these are the first to be attacked. But if all you have are reds and oranges, don't worry—the beetles will find them, too. I've noticed, over the years, that if there are any rugosa roses (species and hybrids) these seem to have the most beetles.

I once was told that old garden roses are exempted from the dietary frenzy of these little feeders. Well, it's not true. Once the beetles are in your garden, they will eat flower and leaf from any rose, regardless of its class or age. A friend in northwestern New York State has long since resigned herself to the fact that the Japanese beetles will prefer to start their dining experience on her gallica and centifolia roses, like hors d'oeuvres at a French restaurant.

Over the years, all kinds of potent and deadly chemicals have been made available with a promise to homeowners that they can rid their gardens of these dinner guests from hell. But you have to have a pretty good aim and a quick eye, because unless the sprays actually hit the beetle, they don't work.

A YEAR OF ROSES

There are safer and still effective alternatives. Studies with adult beetles have shown that when neem oil is applied to the roses as a *foliar* spray, the beetles actually loose their appetite. It's necessary to apply the neem spray on a weekly basis, starting as soon as you see your first beetle. And, you need to sacrifice some of your rose plant as well in order for this spray to work. The beetle has to ingest the foliage sprayed with neem.

Compounds derived from plant sources, including pyrethrums and rotenone, are environmentally friendly (see **August**), and *will* work on Japanese beetles as long as you spray with a very fine mist and spray from the bottom of the plant upward. **Try some companion plantings as a solution for controlling beetles.** Some gardeners claim that Japanese beetles are fatally attracted to four-o'-clocks and larkspur. I do know that these plants are fine companions for roses, so why not try them as a natural control of this pest?

Beetle traps have been around for a long time, and are even enjoying a resurgence as concerns about overuse of chemicals have heightened. I tried these once, and I can report that these traps do indeed work. Up until this point, I had perhaps only a dozen or so beetles—never a problem. But with the traps hanging outside the rose garden, I think every beetle in New York City (and surrounding suburbs) came to inspect the colorful bags. They quickly tired of the crowd scene and went for the roses, and me. I had accidentally rubbed some of the beetle attractant on my nose!

I recently discovered an old family recipe for ridding your garden of Japanese beetles. While trying to wrangle the family marinara sauce recipe from my aunt Marie, I learned instead the secret of my grandmother's beetle repellent.

After the Sunday meal, the men from the old country would sit around the dinner table smoking cigars and eating fennel. Nothing was wasted, as the butts were stored under a tight lid in an ornate ceramic container centered on the dining room table. After a few weeks the juicy stogies were moved to the garage where they continued to ferment in a pail of water.

When the roses came into bloom, the can—now full of mush and exuding a noticeable fragrance—was hung in the rose garden. According to my aunt Marie, there was never a beetle in the rose garden! I never did get her to reveal her recipe for the sauce.

Before flying off, Japanese beetles drop toward the ground when they are threatened. If you hold a can of water under the flower and flick the infested bloom, you'll catch many in this safest of all control techniques. Once the beetle hits the water, it won't go anywhere fast. This is your opportunity: Squash it or decapitate it, then feed it to the birds.

I have gained a great deal of respect for two of the most common birds around, sparrows and seagulls, after learning of their attraction to Japanese beetles.

**One day I actually thought I saw a sparrow grab a Japanese beetle in mid-flight!** To verify, I made myself comfortable and watched some more, as more sparrows congregated in their usual noisy fashion and proceeded to dive-bomb many of the light-colored roses. What few beetles I did have were under vicious attack from these new-found garden allies!

Recently one June, officials at the Atlantic City Airport reported that seagulls were interfering with air traffic at the airport. The gulls were feeding on the Japanese beetles they fond thriving in the tall weeds along the runways. They weren't in fact eating the bugs, but bringing them back to their nests as food for baby seagulls.

Southern gardeners have a substitute for Japanese beetles. The **spotted cucumber beetle**, however, is much more tame by comparison. This beetle is fairly widespread, but the brunt of its damage is mostly felt where mild winters allow them to produce many generations of feeders. This yellow beetle with black spots usually makes its appearance in midspring, after hibernating in the adult stage among the weeds of a garden.

With an inclination to congregate, and often undetected, around the pollen areas of roses, they're more of a problem when you go nose first into the flower for a good sniff! Light mistings of the foliage with neem oil should do the trick with these small beetles, too.

I've heard of potato beetles from friends in Colorado, but I've never had the pleasure of meeting one. Yet another beetle who fancies plant material, the **Colorado potato beetle** is native to the eastern slopes of the Rocky Mountains.

Like the cucumber beetle, It, too, is yellow but with black stripes. This beetle likewise hibernates through the winter as an adult, awakening in the spring with a voracious appetite. If there are no potatoes or other members of the nightshade family (tomatoes, eggplants, petunias, etc.) to dine upon, roses will do. Both the emerging adults and newborn larvae are responsible for destroying foliage. Neem oil should help curb their appetites as well.

Some gardens have what appears to be an ugly cousin of the Japanese beetle—**rose chafer**. Very similar in life cycle, these brown beetles would prefer to skeletonize your rose leaves, rather than the flower. The range of the chafer, which limits itself to areas with sandy soil, is less expansive than the Japanese beetle's. This beetle has been seen in Colorado, but primarily it's found the northeastern regions of our country. There is also a **western rose chafer** found in Arizona and New Mexico.

Rose chafers and Japanese beetles are not the only insects that can skeletonize a rose leaf. **Rose sawflies** are another foliage feeder, and one of the more creative pests in the rose garden.

These wasplike insects are only a problem while in the larval stage. Resembling tiny caterpillars, some are greenish and others are white. Sawfly larvae go under the alias of **rose slugs**. They bear no resemblance to the commonly found slimy garden slugs, but they do share a fondness for the taste of green leaves. Over recent years, I have noticed this pest more and more in my garden (Barnegat, coastal New Jersey) as well as in other gardens throughout the northeast. For me, the rose slugs are far worse than Japanese beetles. Just as the garden is coming into full bloom, many of the shrubs and climbers have nothing but web-like foliage. The entire green part of the leaf is missing. The culprits aren't as easy to locate while this is happening, but if you look closely you'll soon come across the tiny inchworm pest.

**Sawflies** of various types can be found throughout most of the country and are easy to spot because of the damage they do to the plant—and not just by eating its foliage. Some rose slugs bore holes down the center of the rose canes, usually one larva per cane.

Early in the season, the adult female cuts a slice into a leaf (hence the name sawfly) and lays eggs in the leaf tissue. As the roses start coming into bloom, the larvae evolve and begin feeding on the green parts of the leaves. After feeding, the larvae drop off the bush, remaining in the soil until the following spring when they will emerge as adult sawflies. There is usually only one generation of leaf-eating slugs each season, though some seasons might have as many as five. The feeding phase is usually completed as the first flush of bloom comes to an end.

One safe, nonchemical way to control the leaf feeders would be to blast the slugs off the foliage with water. Once they're off the plant, they aren't capable of crawling back on.

If you have a rose infestation way out of control, and the water method proves to be impractical, try spraying the foliage with neem oil or an insecticide containing rotenone. The larvae will be poisoned as they consume the leaves. There is also a possibility that a bacteria such as *Bacillus thuringiensis* (var. *kurstaki*) could be used to kill larvae on the plant and in the soil.

Have I put you off entirely from growing roses? I hope not. These insects aren't as overpowering in populations as it might sound. With the exception of Japanese beetles, you might be hard-pressed to find many of these in your garden. But I thought you should be prepared in case you get an unexpected package in June from a rosarian friend in New Jersey.

I can offer you a perfect solution to guarantee pest-free roses, or at least share with you the novel approach of one gardener in Kansas City: Wrap your roses in fine mesh. Wedding veils will do just fine. Every rose bloom in this garden was carefully shrouded with a lacy veil draped over a tinfoil pie plate attached to a tall wooden stake standing alongside each rose cane. The pie plate formed a perfect shield protecting the rose from the elements. The rosarian was proud of his chemical-free control of beetles. I could only imagine the noise the garden must make each time it rains!

This brings up another type of rose garden denizen—the rose exhibitor.

From Maine to New Mexico, and up to Alaska, amateur rose growers fill buckets, coolers, and portable refrigerators with blooms fresh-cut from their gardens as their roses come into full bloom. These rosarians gather in shopping malls, hotels, churches, botanic gardens, or any place with a table, well before the sun will see their roses. The cut roses have been primped, teased, and coaxed into the most perfect form, and then some.

Convincing a tightly wrapped 'Dolly Parton' to open to the perfect spiral, or getting 'Dainty Bess' to expose her purple stamens with absolute perfection can be a passion bordering on obsession for top rose exhibitors.

Spring rose shows are their annual celebrations of the beauty of the rose, and often the coming-out parties for new rosarians (more like baptism by fire). But they're also a chance to proudly display the results of hard work: all the pruning, fertilizing, and meticulous maintenance of the past months. Most important, these rosarians are sharing their love of roses with everyone who passes by.

Scan your local papers; there's bound to be a rose show for you to visit (or enter) in your area when the roses are starting to bloom. But let me warn you: One blue ribbon, and you're hooked for life!

Unfortunately for a rose exhibitor, the peak of bloom is also the peak of activity for the **leafcutter bee**. This crafty little bee, resembling a bumblebee, cuts perfect half-circles in the foliage of roses, and other garden plants, too. There is nothing you can do about it but admire the ingenuity of these nest-building bees. It should please you to know that out of all the rosebushes in the neighborhood, this bee has chosen yours, lining its nest with pieces of your foliage. Spray all you want, you'll never get them. They work at night, oblivious to your dreams of blue ribbons.

Other enemies of prizewinning roses include sudden rainstorms the day before the show (or worse, hailstorms), causing the spotted or ripped petals scorned mightily by rose judges. Perhaps you've wondered about those colorful cocktail umbrellas mounted lovingly over your neighbor's roses. Now you know. Apart from the rose judges themselves, the unpredictable in nature is often the worst nightmare of a rose exhibitor.

Many times puzzled gardeners wondering if they indeed have a new rose to celebrate have brought me their newly discovered hybrid that seemed to appear overnight in their garden. Here's an example:  A large pink flowering hybrid tea, such as 'Century Two', is suddenly displaying small, blood-red flowers from the same plant that once produced beautiful pink roses. This is especially likely if the rose had been through a harsh winter.  What's happened is a common occurrence with budded plants—rootstock suckering. In this case, 'Century Two' has died over the winter, while the rootstock 'Dr. Huey' survived and is now blooming.

Suckers should be dealt with as soon as they are spotted. A **sucker is simply the rootstock taking over, and if you let it, it will.** Remove the sucker. Otherwise it will deplete the strength of the grafted rose, eventually killing it.

But wait, before you remove anything, make sure it's indeed the rootstock that is suckering. How do you recognize a sucker? For one thing, the foliage and growth habit is noticeably different from the desired rose. Inspect foliage from two different parts of the plant; you should be able to notice a difference right away. Then, of course, there are the different flowers.

On the other hand, suckers originate form *below* the bud union. Those shoots that are growing from the bud union are valuable new basal canes. Save them!

After all this talk of beetles, slugs, and suckers, doesn't June sound wonderful? How about taking time out from doing battle with nature to create more roses from the ones you've nurtured so lovingly? Sharing their favorite roses with friends and neighbors is a time-honored tradition among rosarians of all kinds who know how to propagate roses from cuttings.

You never know when you're going to come upon a rose you've never seen before and can't live without. For me, driving in rose season can be hazardous. I have trouble keeping my eyes on the road when there are roses to be seen. I spy a splash of color. I pull over, lock the car, and follow my nose—my hand gripping my pruning knife while in my backpack are small plastic bags and plenty of moist paper towels. I'm on the prowl—a rose rustler in action.

I wasn't always so bold. It took a few outings with some Texans to get the courage to rustle on my own. I've had interesting experiences, too, knocking on doors and asking permission to take a cutting. Sometimes doors get slammed in my face. Or it can lead to long-winded visits full of childhood recollections of great-grandma's favorite roses. Frequently, I get to take the cuttings—cuttings that will, I hope, eventually be rooted and grown into new shrubs.

Take a 6-inch cutting, either from a branch that has just bloomed, or from a branch that is full of leaves. Label the cutting, giving it a study name or perhaps the person who owns it has a name for this rose already. Wrap the cutting (with leaves and blooms intact) in a dampened towel; put the towel in the plastic bag and seal it. Keep the bag out of the sun. Better yet, if you're really a pro, have a cooler with ice handy to keep the bagged cuttings in while you search for more lost treasures. When you return home you can start rooting the new cuttings.

The cutting can be a straight piece, sliced to a long, chisel-like point. This is the end where you want the new roots to grow. Or you can do what is referred to as a heel cutting: When you make your cutting take some old wood with the new. **This piece of old wood is your heel. With a heel cutting, you want the roots to grow from the old wood, or the heel.** When my volunteers in Brooklyn experimented with growing cuttings from the collection (they were too timid to go rustling), they had the best luck rooting heel cuttings.

I do all my rooting with the help of gallon-sized, sealable plastic sandwich bags and some gritty sand. Fill the bag one-third full of wet (but not dripping) sand. The cutting you want to root should be about four to six inches long. Remove all remains of flowers and leaves except the top set. Make your chisel or heel cutting and insert it into the wet sand. Seal the bag, creating a mini-terrarium. Keep this out of direct sunlight. If you have a clothesline, hang the bagged cutting the way you would your laundry, only in the shade.

In about three weeks you should start to see roots along the bottom of the bag (timing varies from rose to rose). When there are numerous roots visible through the bottom of the bag, pot up the cutting in a small pot and introduce the new plant gradually to the sunnier parts of the garden, don't forget to water the newly potted plant.

By September, you should be able to plant your new rose (which is on its own roots) directly into your garden.

Before leaving the month of June, here's an update on the deer situation in Mom's garden: She's stopped using the garlic powder. Now Mom carefully drapes lightweight netting, of various colors, over her roses in the evening. My sister and I no longer have to bear the lingering odor of a pizza parlor. And, by the way, Mom's roses are beautiful.

---

## RECOMMENDED READING
*Insects That Feed on Trees and Shrubs.* Warren T. Johnson, Howard H. Lyon, C. S. Koehler, J.A. Weidhass. Ithaca, NY. Cornell University Press. 1991.

# July

Why do the weeds have to grow from right through the center of the rosebush? I wonder this as I reach to pull out yet another maple seedling or oxalis growing around the crown of the shrub.

Weeding in the rose garden is a job that's impossible to do without getting scarred. This is the test of good mulch, but even the thickest layers will not prevent at least a few weeds from growing. If the beds were not mulched, the weeds would be out of control by now, because they prosper as the weather gets hotter, and especially when there's less rain. At least the weeds are easier to pull out when the bed is mulched, and I keep reminding myself that a little blood spilt in the garden is good for the roses. Never use weed killers in the rose garden. They can damage the roses.

While you're on hands and knees weeding, what better opportunity to get a close look at your rose bushes? Look beyond the flowers that are still going strong and keep an eye on what's happening in the garden.

With the peak bloom passing, there are few visitors but still many roses in bloom. Most of the once-blooming old roses are finished for the season. How fast they fade depends on how quickly the summer heat arrives. Many varieties of once-blooming old roses prefer long cool springs and summers without scorching heat. I find as soon as the hot summer kicks in that many of these roses start losing their leaves or become prone to black spot. One, for example, is 'Mme. Hardy'. Incredibly beautiful in June, by mid-July her foliage becomes ugly, turning a sort of burnt green. My alba rose 'Alba Suaveolens' looses all its foliage to black spot by the third week of July.

If you have this problem or if your once-bloomers are becoming too big to handle, now is the time to give them a good pruning. Unless the shrub produces a substantial hip display for the autumn, prune a good portion of wood from any of the roses of the following classes: alba, damask, centifo-

**105**

lia, gallica, moss, species, eglantine hybrids, and rugosa hybrids (once and ever-bloomers), and any other modern once-blooming shrub.

Don't prune too much from the hybrid Chinas, hybrid Noisettes, or hybrid Bourbons. These seem to do better if they are pruned in autumn (see **October**).

I've added one ever-blooming shrub rose class to this list because of their tendency to attract spider mites. The hybrid rugosas can stand a pretty drastic thinning out between bloom cycles. Any rose with a rugosa rose parentage tends to suffer badly from spraying –the foliage will burn where the sprays come into contact with it—so I control the pests on these plants with sprays of cold water and pruning. Keeping them thinned makes them much more attractive garden shrubs.

But before pruning any of the above roses, wait until they have reached a fairly good size in the garden. Usually after two growing seasons, there will be enough new growth to warrant a pruning. In their third summer, you can remove about one-third of the plant, always taking away older wood from the center first. Follow through by simply shortening any remaining faded flower stems to a length of 3 or 4 inches.

Try to do this pruning as soon as the flowers have lost their beauty, giving the shrub the rest of the summer to grow new canes for next year's bloom. Depending on how fast these roses grow in your climate, you may want to skip a season, pruning them only every other year.

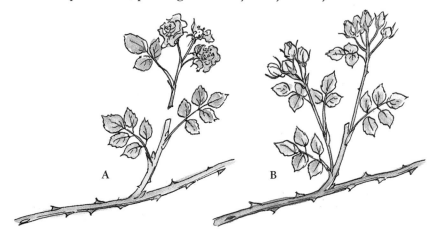

*Repeat blooming shrubs, climbers, and old roses should be deadheaded in order to get the quickest rebloom during a season. Most of these rose types produce blooms on lateral growth.*
*A As you remove the faded bloom, shorten the lateral to two leaves.*
*B Good-sized blooms will be produced from dormant bud eyes along the shortened lateral.*

Hybrid perpetuals, and many of the Bourbon roses, can look pretty bad as soon as hot weather arrives. These I deadhead, shortening the faded flower stems to two or three inches. And if the shrubs are crowded in the center, they get thinned out. I find many of these roses are especially prone to black spot, and they ultimately look best when they have been pruned severely in the early summer. A good watering will encourage strong growth that should return blooms in the autumn.

The Portland roses are still going strong. They'll look good through the entire summer. All they really require right now is regular deadheading. 'Rose de Rescht' and "MacGregor's Damask" are two of my favorite Portlands.

Some of you may be wondering about "MacGregor's Damask", a rose that I love and continue to recommend. If you look for this on any rose list, it seems to have disappeared—but not really. It's one of those classic "rose mysteries" that make for entertaining and heated arguments at a rose society meeting. In this case, it's the east coast versus the west coast.

As it turns out, this rose sold to me in 1985 by a New Hampshire nursery as "MacGregor's Damask" was identical to a rose named "Glendora". "Glendora" apparently was a study name for this rose assigned by the Californian rosarians who discovered it in the Mother Lode country of California. It seems that someone named MacGregor sent cuttings of "Glendora" to New Hampshire, where it became known as "MacGregor's Damask"—apparently the study named assigned to this rose by the New Hampshire nursery. Today (2005), Californian rosarians still stick with the name "Glendora" and refuse to acknowledge any other. While in the east, the name "MacGregor's Damask" has undergone two changes. The first change was to 'Joasine Hanet' (apparently from a resemblance of "MacGregor's Damask" to a 19th century image of a long lost rose 'Joasine Hanet'), but now is seems that 'Joasine Hanet' is again passé. In recent years, a new rose name has been assigned to this rose of great mystery. If you purchase a rose by the name of 'Amanda Patenude', you are in possession of the rose I refer to as "MacGregor's Damask". And since it behaves so wonderfully in my garden, I like to think that it's a Portland rather than a hybrid perpetual (as the Californians claim). So, the mystery continues. . .

The teas and Chinas are just beginning to show their potential. The tea roses area producing a few shy flowers right now, but some of the China roses are quite amazing. Their will to grow is remarkable. Every winter in my garden, "Belfield", a tiny red China rose from Bermuda, is killed to the ground. It's now 8 or 9 inches high, and full of the simple red flowers. Another Bermuda orphan, "Bermuda's Kathleen" (thought to be a seedling of the impressive 'Mutabilis'), is also a beauty. I expect to see more from these roses as the summer bears down on us.

When any ever-blooming shrub or climber goes into a blooming lull, remove some of the older wood and shorten the laterals (the smaller branches that just bloomed). Freestanding shrubs like English roses and hybrid musks should be shaped to give the most attractive appearance.

One of the most impressive displays of a single rose cultivar in the Cranford is a planting of the hybrid musk 'Clytemnestra' bordering a pond. The natural spreading habit of this rare rose makes a beautiful presentation as it spills into the water. In early July, the profusion of apricot-tinted blooms is intensified by its reflection. As the blooms begin to fade in mid-July, I remove the stiffer older wood, allowing the new growth to arch over freely, and I shorten the remaining flowering branches. In a few weeks, 'Clytem-nestra' will begin blooming again, continuing on until frost. (Sadly, this planting from 1935 has been replaced with the newer shrub rose 'Knockout').

If your ever-blooming climbers such as 'New Dawn, 'Inspiration', and 'Mermaid' are starting to get out of control, remove older canes to make room for the new ones.

However, there are still some roses that haven't bloomed yet. For instance, the North American native rose *Rosa setigera* (or the 'Prairie Rose') will only just begin to bloom around the second week in July. This perhaps comes closest of all the roses to becoming a natural climbing plant. Originally found throughout the Eastern Seaboard and the Prairie States, this scentless pink beauty creates mounds of color and is best left alone on an embankment or in an open field where it can sprawl.

Another late-blooming species of note is not an American native but hails from the Far East. Also needing a great deal of space, *Rosa wichurana* is best described as a natural creeping rose, hugging close to the ground with wonderfully fragrant white flowers supported by shiny, disease-resistant foliage. Also known as the 'Memorial Rose', it was initially used in America as a living grave blanket, unaffected by diseases common to garden roses and a habit perfect for decorating graves. But after a year or two, cemetery caretakers found it impossible to find the tombstones! Banished from graveyards, *Rosa wichurana* was instantly initiated into the world of rose breeding.

These two species roses, along with another oriental native, *Rosa mul-tiflora*, were responsible for the development of a new group of roses known collectively as ramblers.

Their extremely rangy offspring are still popular today, coming into their peak of bloom in Brooklyn during early July just as the modern shrub-type roses are beginning to fade. "Rambler" is descriptive of their natural growth habit. The new growth tends to be in the form of long, pliable canes, often starting from the base of the plant, but also from higher up the old wood.

Quite often, ramblers send out fountains of growth while in bloom, sometimes detracting from the beauty of this shrub, and giving them the appearance of a tangled mass of green growth and flowers. They also require a great deal of space if left to grow on their own. This earns them a reputation for being difficult.

Chances are, if you drive through any small town, hike along an old railroad bed, or clear way the tangle of weeds in the rear of your new piece of property, you may come across a rambler growing without any care at all.

These roses are survivors. Large feet, lawnmowers, even the occasional disaster can't stop them. When returning to her property that had been completely destroyed by hurricane Katrina, a glimmer of hope greeted my friend Peggy. A pink rambler was in bloom, named "Louisiana Rambler" by local rosarians since it is found in great abundance naturalized throughout the gulf region of this state. In Natchez, Mississippi, I discovered a rustic barn that had shifted off of its foundation many years before. Bursting through a broken windowpane was 'Dorothy Perkins' in glorious bloom, on both sides of the glass! This rambler, sheared to the ground when the barn shifted, was now growing from inside the barn. The unorthodox pruning had rejuvenated a neglected plant.

Find the right place in your garden to grow a rambler. How you use a rambler in the garden will determine the amount of work it requires of you.

The easiest way to grow a rambler is to allow it all the room in the world to grow. Let it spill down an embankment, cover a rocky shoreline, or even mound up to create a hedgerow. If you have an open field, it would be beautiful to let this rose grow into its natural habit: a mound of color in midsummer. This design would require no care at all. This is how you may find them in the wild, abandoned for many decades.

In most gardens, however, ramblers are used in a decorative fashion, covering fences, arbors, and arches to highlight the shape of a structure, or as a backdrop to a garden. There are many uses in this style, and this is where ramblers earn their reputation as difficult roses to grow. It doesn't take long before a pink beauty like 'Dorothy Perkins' become a nightmare of black spot, mildew, and spider mites. The solution is easy: Prune this rambler—and any other that is quickly outgrowing its space.

Unless you have an exceptionally aggressive grower and it's taking over more space than you had planned for it, don't prune your ramblers the first year in your garden. They may not bloom, but they will grow.

*Ramblers and climbers look best when spiraled around an arch.*

What is growing this season will be producing flowers next year, so save as much of the growth as possible. Train the canes as they are produced, bending and wrapping them around the structure. Take advantage of the pliable nature of the canes. But during the first summer of a rambler's life, only prune what has become a nuisance.

It's during the second year, and every year after, that you will begin to see your patience paying off. Ramblers become more beautiful as they age. They also sprout new canes like weeds every summer. Now it's time to make that cut.

The easiest way to start is simply to deadhead the plant. When you do this, shorten every faded flower stem to a new length of three inches. With the laterals shortened, you will be able to make more sense of the growth habit.

Next, take another look at the plant. Are there new shoots? If so, locate their origins. Many are probably from the base, but some are very likely to be growing from old wood. This is an important observation to make when it comes time to cut the older growth. You don't want to make the mistake of cutting anything that is supporting a beautiful new cane.

Remove as much of the old wood as you can. Sometimes all the old wood goes, but only if there is enough new wood to take its place. Otherwise, save enough of the old to maintain your desired design.

If I'm growing a rambler along a fence (3 feet high), I save eight canes. I train four toward the right side of the fence and the remaining four to the left. I always make sure that the canes are curved. It's fun to make use of the pliable nature of these roses.

Ramblers look great on narrow arches (3-inch iron bands, for instance). Leave just three canes wrapped around each band after pruning.

There are many uses for these roses in your garden, but to ensure the most enjoyment possible from them, you shouldn't be afraid to cut them. Besides looking bad, unpruned ramblers attract the **Two-spotted spider mite**.

Thanks to the era of DDT use in gardens, spider mites enjoyed a population explosion. This infamous pesticide killed off many of the insects that preyed upon the mites.

As if overnight, spider mites will populate the garden when the conditions are right. In July, the potential is there: hot weather with very little rainfall. Add to this a crowded plant and any hot reflective surface and you've got a winning combination.

**Spider mites are not insects.** They are in the same family as spiders and ticks. There are many different types of these tiny pests, the most common one in the garden being the Two-spotted variety. Often called red spider mites, or simply red spiders, they have the appearance of tiny specks of paprika on the underside of the foliage.

An infestation is evident when the lower foliage of your roses starts to turn dusty-yellow or even gray. If you're not sure, hold a leaf under a hand lens and you'll see the mites. When the population is out of control, you will actually see webbing from leaf to leaf.

My miniature roses are growing in a semicircular bed backed by a hedge of Japanese holly and fronted by a blue stone and brick terrace. Until this year, the hedge was two and a half feet high. This created a microenvironment, limiting the air movement through the roses. The stone terrace reflects a great deal of heat, and spider mites love this. I consider the roses in this bed to

*Spider Mite*

be my indicator plants for spider mites. When it's time for mites, I'll see them here first.

Spider mites don't arrive overnight. By the time you notice them, they've had a long life in your garden. They hibernate as adults through the winter in protected spots: under eaves, on leaves of evergreen shrubs and weeds (violets, for one), and under bark of trees, in the crevices of a wall garden, or in the soil. In late winter or early spring, when the temperatures reach the mid-fifties, mites begin to populate.

Hundreds of eggs are laid on the undersides of the leaves, occurring more frequently as the temperature begins to rise. The hotter the temperature, the faster a mite reaches its mature stage. In the early spring, for example, a mite will take as long as forty days to reach maturity, while in warmer weather (above 75 degrees Fahrenheit) it can take as little as five days to mature from egg to adult. The orgies are beginning to peak in July and will last as long as the conditions are favorable.

Give them a cold shower. Blast them right off the bush with a hose, making sure you thoroughly wet the undersides of the leaves. Daily misting will continue to interrupt their pleasurable existence. Prune away cluttered growth—especially from the center of the plant—get rid of those twiggy branches, and by all means get rid of any part of the plant that is covered in webs.

There are different pesticides available to destroy the adults. But make sure the chemical is a miticide and also follow through in five to seven days to get the next generation that will have hatched. I have had excellent luck through continual cold-water treatments together with pruning. In severe situations, highly refined horticultural oils (such as Sunspray Oil) will do the job, too. There are several predatory mites specifically hungry for Two-spotted spider mites. These mites are available from many mail-order sources.

To discourage the problem in the first place, look around the garden and determine what can be altered to create a less desirable situation. I clipped my hedge very low to improve air circulation and I'm considering getting rid of the hedge entirely. Remove any weeds from the beds. Certain weeds are particularly inviting to mites: violets, pokeweed, Jerusalem oak, Jimsonweed, wild blackberry, and oxalis.

**Black spot** will begin to show its true ugliness by the time the first peak of roses has come to an end. Every year I think that maybe this year I have it beat. Then suddenly leaves are showing the telltale black spots, and before I know it, they're turning yellow and falling off.

Some roses are very tolerant of black spot, getting only a small amount of the disease. Others are black spot magnets. But no rose is completely immune, and the black spots, for which it is named, will start appearing as soon as high humidity and high temperatures arrive.

One thing I can guarantee I that black spot will show up on *any* rose that is watered in the evening. If the foliage is wet for at least six hours, it's a perfect situation for the fungus to enter a leaf. Also, avoid working in the garden if the plants are wet. If there are spores around, you can unknowingly carry and spread the disease when moving from one wet plant to another.

Roses under stress, such as from lack of water or too much fertilizer, are likely to become infected. The same can be said for roses growing too closely together.

Black spot is not a new disease and doesn't only infect modern roses. It has its roots in old garden roses, and was first recorded in 1815, in Sweden[1]. For all for all of you who like to point fingers of blame at hybrid teas for causing this disease, note that this was fifty-two years *before* the creation of the hybrid tea class.

One species rose in particular, *Rosa foetida*, shows an amazing attraction to the disease. A great many of our modern-day yellow roses are descendants of this rose. If you've grown yellow roses, no doubt you've had black spot. I refer to *Rosa foetida* (also known as 'Austrian Yellow') as the "Typhoid Mary" of the rose world.

The safest and the healthiest method for controlling black spot is through pruning. Get rid of all infected parts. Remove lower foliage 3 to 6 inches up from the ground, as well as twiggy growth, as the first flush of blooms fade. This is a wise preventative, since black spot starts in the lower regions of a rosebush.

Experiments are being conducted using anti-desiccants to control black spot with great success. The infection of a leaf by the black spot fungus occurs through the leaf surface. The role of the anti-desiccants (such as Wilt-Pruf) is to create a protective layer on the leaf and slow the loss of moisture through transpiration. It is thought that perhaps this same protective layer can prevent fungi from getting into the leaf tissue. Similar experiments are being conducted in Texas with organic fertilizers sprayed on the foliage as a method of controlling the spread of this disease. Many rosarians have had success in using neem oil as a fungicide, as well. Check with your local extension agent and rose society for updates on these and other experimental methods of controlling black spot.

Spraying or dusting with sulfur will help control this disease. Great care should be taken, however, if you decide to use a liquid sulfur spray during July. Temperatures over 85 degrees Fahrenheit can lead to foliage burn.

If all else fails, there are fungicides on the market that will control the spread of black spot when used correctly. And whether you dust with sulfur or spray with a popular fungicide, make sure you get both sides of the leaves with a fine dust or mist.

**With sprays, I have found that the medicine is sometimes worse than the disease.** Leaf burn and defoliation can happen overnight with an overdose of a spray, or if you spray when it's too hot outside. A dry garden can bring on the same results. Follow the directions, and remember—increasing the dosage does not make a fungicide (or any other chemical, for that matter) more effective. It only becomes more lethal to you and to the plants.

Pay attention to the weather. Black spot is more apt to spread after humid evenings and summer rainstorms. When you spray, do it on a regular cycle. Spray every seven to ten days. The cycle depends on which spray you use—always follow the recommendations on the package. Use common sense and refrain from spraying if there is rain in the forecast that day, or during heat waves. I generally won't spray if the temperature is over 90 degrees Fahrenheit, but wait for cooler weather.

If you continue to have black spot problems year after year, you can try moving the roses to a new spot with better air circulation, or consider getting rid of the problem roses and finding a better suited variety. Don't let one or two bad cultivars ruin your rose garden. Avoid planting black spot susceptible types together. The disease will spread with great ease in this situation. You also may want to break up the plantings of roses with other garden plants. I have learned to hide this sin of the rose with companion plants such as: agastache, nepeta, and many other perennials and annuals with small foliage and colorful flowers.

As gardens in upper New England are beginning to enjoy their first flush of color, I prepare to buckle down for a long, hot summer—possible a dry one. This is when I begin to notice something funny with some of the new growth of the roses. If it looks as though the tips of emerging branches have been burned, with a sort of shriveled appearance, this damage suggests that I might have the dreaded **rose midge**.

Look carefully at any branches that aren't blooming or showing signs of new growth. On a piece of affected new growth, peel away the layers of tissue and study them under a hand lens. If you see creamy, sometimes orange, maggots, you have midge. Immediately, cut off all infected parts, bag them up, and throw them into the trash. It's best to assume that the entire plant and garden is populated with this dinner guest. Cut back all non-blooming wood from every rose, at least several inches on each branch.

There are many midges in the insect world. The one that is destructive in the rose garden is simply called *rose midge* (*Dasyneura rhodophaga*)[2], a member of the gall midge family. The adult midge is a very small flying insect, practically impossible to spot with the naked eye. Rose midge lays its eggs in the growing points of the rose plant, inserting them deep into the new developing tissue. The eggs hatch into tiny maggots that feed on the succulent new growth. As they mature over five to seven days, they suck sap from the rose plant. After fattening up, the maggots fall off the plant and into the soil below where they finish their development into a mature midge. The total life cycle from egg to fly could be as short as twelve days. With twenty to thirty eggs hatching on a leafy tissue at one time, these voracious feeders will devour, or distort, the emerging tissue in no time at all.

It's possible that all new leaves and flowers on a single plant will be affected. Sometimes a flower will develop despite the invasion. In this case the bloom emerges with a severely bent neck. Unfortunately, by the time you see the damage it's already too late to control that cycle. However, you can control the spread of this uninvited guest.

Midge is not a new pest, having been around since the late 1880's. Rose midge gained notoriety as a greenhouse pest with florist roses. Somewhere, somehow, it escaped and spread to outside gardens.

Midge over-winters in the garden in a pupal stage, in cocoons buried in the soil. As the temperature warms up, the vicious cycle starts all over again. Midge can remain active nearly up to the first frost. It's the suddenness of their infestation that makes midge so devastating. What was a lush garden full of blooms in June can be reduced rather quickly to just foliage in a few weeks' time.

For a long time the control for rose midge was DDT. Today, many people have had good results with diazinon or Merit (both are **granular pesticides** applied to the soil in the spring to kill the emerging pupae), but I refuse to add this to my garden. I worry about the long lasting effects of a granular pesticide in the garden, especially if it gets into the water table. Instead, I have had good results using a pyrethroid insecticide as a weekly spray during infestations. The particular pyrethroid, cyfluthrin, is scheduled to be available in the very near future under (hopefully) a friendlier name. Bayer Agricultural Products is one company that has recently released an insecticide containing this compound, for the home gardener. Check with your local garden center.

Other gardeners I know have been experimenting with beneficial nematodes in the soil to attack the larval-pupal stage. One nematode that might find the larvae of rose midge tasty is *Hydronmermis conopophaga*[3].

To be effective, this has to be applied as a soil drench in early spring and in the autumn. The friendly nematode needs a couple of seasons to show some results. Still more research and studies are desperately needed in dealing with this pest.

There are no roses that appear to be immune to midge, with the exception of climbing roses. My guess is that the midge doesn't like to travel very high. All damage seems to be at eye level or lower.

A few words of advice: If you've had midge before, it won't suddenly go away on its own. You should be on the lookout for a repeat of the problem next season, as early as the first signs of growth on your rosebushes.

Gardeners way up north in the cold zones from the Dakotas to upper Michigan are lucky to not have to deal with problems like thrips, downy mildew, or maybe even Japanese beetles. The cold winters keep these pests at bay. However, you might see one of the ugliest critters ever to attack a rose, the **rose curculio** (probably the most difficult to pronounce, too).

The rose curculio actually prefers the colder regions of our country. It's a small black or reddish-brown beetle with a very long snout. Spending the early part of the rose season among the species roses or fruit brambles, it will descend upon the modern roses, as the flower buds are ready to open. It bores with its snout into the flower buds before they open. To make matters worse, it can also lay its eggs inside the flower bud, causing the bloom to be destroyed as it opens.

Most of the time you don't see the beetle, just the holes. Not having had the pleasure of experiencing them firsthand, I can only suggest trying neem oil or perhaps a pyrethrum-based spray.

July presents many challenges for the rosarian. Between the black spot, spider mites, and midge, you have your hands full. True, when the temperatures start rising we begin to see an increase in the activity of these problems. Despite all of these inconveniences, there are still wonderful roses to enjoy. As August nears, you might want to begin to think about selecting more roses, replacing some, or figuring out exactly where you can expand you rose garden.

[1]Westcott, *Westcott's Plant Disease Handbook*. 4th ed. New York: Van Nostrand Reinhold Company, 1979.

[2]Metcalf, *Destructive and Useful Insects: Their Habit and Control*. 2nd ed. New York: McGraw-Hill Book Company, Inc, 1939.

[3]William Olkowski, *Common Sense Pest Control*. Newton, CT.: The Taunton Press, 1991.

# AUGUST

A ugust is the month rosarians lock their garden gates and throw away the key. I can remember peaking over a wall one August after I had promised the owner, a collector of old roses, that I wouldn't go anywhere near her garden that day. She was mortified that I would even consider visiting her in August. This was the very same person who had accused me years earlier of killing 'Ophelia' (I had since learned that 'Ophelia' was indeed a rose, a rather pathetic-looking one at that).

I honored her request. But after I ran into her at a local shopping mall, how could I resist the temptation? I carefully tiptoed through the poison ivy between the road and her garden, avoiding the garden gate, to get a disappointing—but ever so fulfilling—peek over the wall. Not a rose in bloom, and not too much in the foliage department, either. So much for the indestructible beauty of old roses! Wasn't it only natural that I wondered about the state of *her* 'Ophelia'?

As extreme and varied as the cold weather in January is, the same can be said of the hot days of August all over the country. Add to this the humidity and the inevitable drought, and you have the wrong recipe for roses, Well, not all roses resent this weather, but August is definitely a test for roses *and* the rosarian.

**August is about patience, persistence, and hygiene.** Persistence, because you have to keep on with the seemingly mundane chores of deadheading, watering, and weeding to keep the garden looking its best; hygiene, because it's the time for every possible disease and pest to be invading your garden, and the best defense is a clean garden; and patience, because you know that very soon autumn will arrive with its cooler weather—bringing relief and lots of new roses.

After the showy displays of roses all spring and through July, you might notice a sudden decrease in new blooms. There is more to it than just talk when you hear about summer dormancy. When it gets really hot, most roses go into a rest phase. This is the norm for the Deep South, or anywhere that has prolonged periods of heat. Gardeners in New Orleans and Charleston don't just think in terms of winter dormancy. Instead, a summer dormant period is an important part of their gardening cycle as well.

Plant hardiness, a term found in all gardening books and plant catalogues, is determined by two things: the plants ability to survive cold and heat. The lowest temperature a plant can endure determines the cold hardiness of that plant. Many years ago, the USDA created a plant hardiness map using the average coldest temperatures recorded within the different areas of our country as its criteria. At that time eleven zones were designated, Zone 1 being the coldest with an average minimal low temperature of –50 degrees Fahrenheit, and Zone 11 the warmest with an average minimum temperature of 40 degrees Fahrenheit. Over the years, this information has been updated with zones 2 through 10 subdivided into a and b creating a total of twenty different cold hardiness zones. This map still serves as the guide used when discussing the zone hardiness of a plant.

These zones should be taken as reference points only and you should be aware of variations within each. Fluctuations in temperatures can make

*It's important to keep up with the deadheading since faded blooms can look unsightly and breed diseases.*

a significant difference in the survival of a plant. How quickly the cold weather happens and whether or not it remains consistently cold makes a difference. Winter thaws could also be critical factors in determining whether or not a plant is going to survive the winter.

The colder a zone, the shorter the growing season. My experiences have proven that in the areas of shorter seasons, the plants seem to grow faster and more vigorously as if to get as much gusto out of the cooler weather. In cold zones, Gardeners tend to do most of their planting in the spring after the danger of a freeze has passed. However, if you have at least a month of autumn, I would recommend planting in the autumn. The soil is still warm, there's usually plenty of rain, and the plants are always marked at a discount! It would be advisable to mulch the plants after a freeze to keep them consistently cold during the winter.

Many plants have the natural ability to go dormant to protect them from winter. Those with this ability are categorized as cold hardy plants. Deciduous shrubs and trees lose their leaves and essentially shut down their system. All roses except for teas and Chinas have this natural ability to go dormant. Perennials can do two things—either store their food in the roots and die to ground level each autumn, or drop their foliage and spend the winter in the garden as a dormant woody skeleton. Annuals complete their life cycles each season, and scatter their seeds for next season. Some plants, like daffodils, tulips, and lilies store everything in a bulb deep in the ground during winter.

Until recently, the ill effects of heat to plants had been ignored. Failure in the garden due to heat and confusion caused by the zone system of the cold hardiness map gave cause to the creation of the American Horticultural Society's heat zone map. In a similar design to the cold hardiness map, the heat zone map is divided into twelve zones. The zones are determined by the average number of days a region may experience temperatures over 86 degrees Fahrenheit, the temperature when plants start to display significant signs of heat stress. These are referred to as heat days and zone 1, the coldest, has an average of 1 heat day (the highest peaks of the Rockies, for example) while zone 12, the hottest, could average at least 210 heat days (the lower southwest corner of Florida and Texas). This information is especially helpful for gardeners in the south and the southwest, the two hottest regions of our country.

Are you growing the right roses for your garden? This is a good question to ask yourself now as the summer heat can make them look their worst. Any rose that continually gives you problems—too much dieback in the winter, too much black spot in the summer—and requires a great deal of pampering might not be the rose for your. There are roses out there that are right for your garden; it's even possible that some will thrive with limited spraying or none at all. August is the time to find them.

I keep one area of the garden as carefree as possible, not intentionally, but more because it's just always out of reach. There is a steep hillside facing the Cranford Rose Garden that was actually contained within the original design of the garden, but never really utilized until recently. I started planting 'orphans" from the main collection here—mainly hybrid teas and floribunda roses without name tags. Eventually, I started adding plantings of the new shrub roses flooding the market: English roses, the new Canadian hybrids known as Explorer roses, the numerous new hybrids from the Carefree collection ('Carefree Delight', 'Wonder', etc.), the Meidiland hybrids ('Alba Meidiland', 'Red Meidiland', etc.)—all the new "fads" eventually made it to this developing garden, as well as many old garden roses. I grew many of these roses in the main garden, as well, where they were  pruned to keep them from interfering with neighboring varieties. My intent for the hillside plantings was to let these roses go— not quite wild, but to the point where they could attain their most natural shape and size.

Out of reach of my irrigation system, out of mind when I spread my monthly fertilizer (I do give them a spring boost), and, as I'm usually not interested in spraying them for pests, these roses are virtually left on their own. A case study of abused and neglected roses.

Despite this treatment, they do get full sun, they enjoy a very rich, well-drained organic soil, and they do get pruned. I give my annual beginner's pruning class here, and then my volunteers follow through and clean up.

The results are very interesting. Planted without a planting design, there is a sort of Monet-like quality about the garden in June: an Impressionist's canvas coming to life. As formal a the main garden is, this is the wild side of the collection, and it's becoming my favorite. Judging by the amount of visitors who wander up through the shrubs, it's becoming a favorite of others, too.

By August, perhaps 30 percent of this garden looks alive. The Meidiland shrubs on the steepest slopes are superb, the Explorers are holding their foliage, the Carefree roses need a good pruning, and some of the English roses are indeed showing a high disease resistance. But then again, these don't have any foliage left, so how could they have any diseases?

As I look out over the hillside, among the roses in absolutely glorious bloom, with foliage intact, are: 'Graham Thomas', 'Abraham Darby', 'Heritage' (these three are of the English group), 'Sally Holmes', 'Spartan', 'Frau

Karl Druschki', 'Sadlers Wells', 'The Fairy', 'White Cap', 'Carefree Wonder', 'Prosperity', 'Pink Princess', 'Rhonda', and 'Rose de Rescht'.

There are many once-blooming old roses that are looking good, too, with lots of lush foliage and some developing hips. From my vantage point, I can see 'Duc de Guiche', *Rosa wichurana*, 'Alain Blanchard', 'Oeillet Flamand', and 'Maiden's Blush'.

I think it's only fair to warn you: Beware of Shakespeare. Many of the roses in one collection bearing the names from this author's works seem to be doomed. As much as I love the colors and fragrances of 'Othello', 'Fair Bianca', and 'Prospero', these are nothing right now but sticks in the garden. But this is not limited to just these roses, for the same can be said of other popular varieties such as 'Baronne Prévost', 'Paul Neyron', 'Chicago Peace', 'Gypsy Carnival', 'Country Dancer', and 'Double Delight'.

Besides the neglect, one common factor among all of the above roses is that they are growing on 'Dr. Huey' rootstocks. Their poor performance is a further indication to me that perhaps the problem is related to the rootstock, not the individual variety. I have tried these again as both own-root plants and as plants budded onto *Rosa multiflora*. The improvement was remarkable, especially with the English varieties. I now only grow and recommend these beauties if they are on their own roots or budded onto *Rosa multiflora* (for cold climates) or budded onto 'Fortuniana' (for warm climates and Florida).

These observations are based on what occurred in this particular garden, free from care. There are many roses that could survive this. I know of many hybrid teas I could add to the hill. 'Peaudouce' (aka 'Elina'), 'Maid of Honour', and 'Esther Geldenhuys' are three I can think of immediately. Another hybrid tea of high merit is 'Curly Pink'. This pink and fragrant (one of the strongest fragrances among the hybrid teas) cultivar is never without blooms—from June through December. But there are other hybrid teas I would recommend, as well as many varieties from other classes.

In recent years, some very interesting work is being conducted in the search for truly carefree roses for the garden. One in particular is the National Earthkind Rose Research Program, a study sponsored by Texas A&M University and the Houston Rose Society. Cultivars of roses, modern and old, are being grown and evaluated by rosarians, professional and amateur, throughout our country with the hopes of establishing a list of rose varieties that are truly carefree in all climates. As of May 2005, countless organizations and individuals in twenty-three states, including three major botanic gardens, were participating in the national research project. The plan is to expand to all fifty states and Canada in the year 2006.

These roses are grown with minimal care and evaluated primarily for disease resistance, cold hardiness, and heat tolerance. Those selected from these trials will be marketed as Earthkind roses. So far, leading the list as Earthkind Roses are: 'Mutabilis', 'Belinda's Dream', and many of the Griffith Buck hybrids.

Besides the blooming characteristics of my roses on the hill, I was able to pay attention to the truer growth style of these roses since they were not as heavily pruned. Besides the lull in blooming, there is another reaction to the heat that can cause disappointment in your garden. Some roses have an abundance of vegetative growth with less blooms. This has been my experience with many of the English shrub roses that have been introduced in the last few years.

The first season the I grew the English roses (also known as David Austin Roses) I was greatly puzzled by their growth habits. I would guess that these new roses were unaccustomed to the heat and humidity typical of our summers. In the catalog, the predicted growth habit for 'Graham Thomas' was 5 feet high by 4 feet wide. In the first summer, my plant had nearly doubled that and was still growing. This wasn't unique to one cultivar alone, but to many. I checked with other gardens and reactions were similar. There was a great deal of vegetative growth brought on by the heat.

This same pattern of growth will occur if you grow cold-hardy old roses—gallicas, albas, damasks—in hot climates. It seems that they, too, react to the extra heat with very vigorous vegetative growth, disappointing to gardeners who fall in love with these roses previously only through catalogs and books.

Make a list of roses in your garden that do really poorly and those that look good. Visit other gardens in August: an old cemetery, a public garden, or your neighbors'. Perhaps there was a rose that you saw in June that you thought you couldn't live without. Why not go back and see if it still has that effect on you. If in August you still love those same roses you saw in June, then these are the roses for you to grow. Also, find out what kind of maintenance program the garden you're visiting has. Do they spray regularly or not? (Most public gardens use a fairly strict regimen of pesticides to keep the gardens looking as nice as possible.) There is bound to be a garden somewhere where you can find out just exactly how the roses do with limited care.

August is the worst month for a rosebush, and the best time to critique them—when they're looking less than perfect.

Don't be put off by a rose that is not in bloom. At this time of year, I pay attention to the growth potential. Consider the foliage. Older leaves should be an even green color, and new foliage can be green and/or red. I get a great sense of satisfaction when I look over an August rose bed an see red foliage supporting small flower buds. In a few weeks I know there will be blooms everywhere.

A visit to a rose exhibitor's garden in August might shake you up a bit. Exhibitors who are planning on showing prize blooms in the autumn rose shows prune in early August, or even by the end of July.

An exhibitor's pruning at this time of year might be as severe as spring pruning. Their goal is to get as big a rose as possible with the longest stem for best exhibition.

I prune now, but I do it mainly for black spot control as well as for rejuvenation. I look at August as the month of falling leaves: rose leaves turning yellow and falling off. There could be a variety of causes—heat, drought damage from overfertilizing, mites—but most likely it's from black spot. Black spot is probably the number one reason behind the yellowing of your rose leaves. It usually reaches its peak of infestation in my garden as the dog days of summer sneak in and stay for the month of August.

I'm not ashamed of the fact that I have black spot. It just can't be avoided. Besides, what's a little black spot between friends?

When your spray program fails you (be careful of what you spray in the hot weather), come to your senses and prune your bushes.

Any repeat blooming shrub that is not in bloom and not looking healthy should be cut. How far back to prune is up to you. Remember, the farther you cut back the rosebush, the longer it will take for the plant to rebloom. If you have a cluster of one variety planted together, prune some of them more severely than others to stagger the late summer-autumn bloom.

When you prune, remove as much wood as it takes to give the plant some sort of shape that you find attractive—or at least bearable. Sometimes I cut up to one-third of the existing plant, especially with hybrid teas and floribundas. Other times, If I simply can't stand the way a rosebush looks with no flowers and no leaves, I'll mow it down. An example of this is my polyantha 'Baby Faurax'. By the end of July, just as the serious heat kicks in, my five plants of this magenta rose are a collection of ugly little sticks in the garden, no foliage at all. They happen to edge the bed, within easy reach of the lawn mower. By September they recover and start blooming a new.

Speaking of polyanthas, I have noticed that those on their own root system are in superb form, full of blooms and foliage (this seems to be true of many roses from other classes that are on their own roots as well). But particularly those polyanthas that are grafted are not faring well in this heat ('Baby Faurax', for example).

*Black spot quickly causes the leaves to turn yellow and fall off.*

Gardeners in the southern states and the Southwest, where temperatures can reach an excessive degree of heat, should wait until the weather cools before pruning. The fresh tissue exposed during pruning can be burned. Wait until the autumn.

Black spot is not the only fungus-related disease that can be problematic now. Perhaps you've noticed some of your roses suddenly wilting, random branches turning black, or dying back from the tip. In addition to the wilting/dieback, you might see some large blotches that gradually encircle canes. Canes with these blotches eventually die, too.

There are many different fungi that become active in the garden during stressful times caused by drought, heat dormancy, improper nutrition, etc., when the plants' defenses are at a minimum. The results of the damage caused by these various fungi are usually grouped under the simple, descriptive heading of **dieback.**

Any canker lesion left on the plant during spring pruning will cause dieback. Other specific fungal diseases such as **anthracnose**, or **wilt**, cause dieback. Dieback can also happen as a result of sawfly and stem girdler damage.

I notice dieback happening regularly with my rugosa roses (among the hybrids as with the species) and often in the species roses *Rosa carolina*, *Rosa canina*, and *Rosa multiflora*. I don't see it as regularly among my modern shrubs, but when I do, there tends to be more of it with roses on their own root systems.

The differences among many of the fungal diseases are subtle and how they got into your garden can be a mystery, but it's not always a mystery. Perhaps you overlooked problems on some of the canes during spring pruning. It's also possible that a new rose you planted in spring or summer was infected. It doesn't take much for these fungi to spread and make themselves at home. The causes can be difficult to pinpoint, but it's easy to create the right environment for them to spread.

It's important to remember that all fungi travel with water, spreading easily by splashing water onto the foliage of the roses. If you see dieback or any fungus-caused disease in your garden, be very careful how you water your garden. At the same time, make sure that your watering system is working, giving the roses enough water. Lack of water will create a stressful situation, ideal for the spread of diseases.

Fungi will also find safe harbor in any deadwood left on the plants. Take time this month to examine all of your roses and remove all deadwood and stubby growth.

While working in your garden, be extra careful that you don't wound any of the canes, even slightly. Any breaks in the wood will provide an open door for fungi and insects looking for easy nests. This warning is especially important to heed if you cultivate your soil.

Finally, excessive use of fertilizers will produce too much succulent growth. Heavy-handed doses of nitrogen are often the direct cause of problems like these in the garden.

There is a small pest that could also cause sudden die back. San Jose scale is not too easy to spot unless you are nose to thorn with a rose bush, and if you're pruning in August, or in the spring, you may want to check for signs of this insect. Found in gardens throughout our country, this scale is related to the rose scale I find in my species roses in the winter, but instead of white, it has a dark scale, nearly black, which should be visible at this time. Like with the rose scale, the best control is through pruning and using horticultural oils or lime-sulfur sprays.

A poor bud union can also be the cause of many a rose's failing, especially in the heat of August. Sloppy grafting techniques in the growing fields of the nursery that propagates the rose or a virus in the plant can cause a budded rose to die suddenly to the bud union.

If the health of the rose is consistently poor (continual yellowing leaves, dieback of new growth, blackening of canes) and you don't see any visitors to the foliage, or wounds in the canes, it's time to remove the rose and look at the parts of the plant that have been underground. The roots of any plant are probably its most overlooked area, but if the roots aren't healthy, you'll never have healthy growth.

The first thing I would do is check the soil. With a spading fork, probe into the ground. The soil should not be wet and mucky as you dig up the plant. The tool should be able to penetrate the soil easily as you dig. If this is not the case, then you have your first clue to what is going wrong.

Remove the plant and look at the roots. Don't expect a massive root ball, in the likes of a tree or a forsythia bush. If you have a rose on its own root system, a root ball is a possibility, but the root system of most roses, especially one that's been in the ground for a long time, is more likely to be open and less likely to hold soil as you remove it from the ground.

Examine the shape of the root system. It should be extending in all directions, multibranched. A healthy root system should have many small feeder roots coming off the older, thicker ones. These smaller roots are the important roots, the ones that absorb the nutrients and water, making your roses grow. An absence of the fine roots indicates that the soil is lacking a good particle quality, or in other words, it is not aerated enough.

If it looks as though the rose has been growing in a pot (roots wrapped around each other—thicker outer roots tightly wrapped around thinner feeding roots), this is not good, especially if you originally had planted a bare-root plant. Even if you originally planted this rose from a container, the root system should have broken from the original pattern of the container. If not, then these signs indicate that the soil in your garden is not encouraging root growth outward, away from the crown of the plant. Roots will always grow in the path of least resistance. Fortunately, these are all problems that are easy to amend.

Add more bulky organic, such as chips, to your soil. Cultivate the soil around the base of the rose, mixing in more chips and creating a looser soil to enable the root system to grow outward and into the garden. If you have a large bed of roses, and they are all exhibiting poor growth, then it might be practical to excavate the entire bed, or at least amend the soil for all of the roses.

Look closely at the actual roots. Inspect for **root gall** and **crown gall**. They will appear as little cauliflower-like growths on the roots or around the area where the soil level was. These galls, just like stem gall (see **March**), reduce the vigor of the rose and eventually kill it if you don't remove them. These are soil borne diseases, so get rid of the soil the rose was growing in.

One very obvious problem that results from poor aeration and overwatering is **root rot**. A dead giveaway to root rot is an obnoxious smell from the soil as you remove the rosebush. The roots are dead or dying, and when you handle the roots, you can easily peel way layers of tissue and the roots crumble or turn to mush.

Root rot is brought on in a number of ways. In some parts of the country there are specific bacteria that can cause root rot. It can be the result of generally poor soil conditions. Or perhaps nematodes are the culprit (see **September**).

One cause of root rot is excessive watering—especially from lawn watering systems or any system that ends up sending too much water into the rose beds. I encountered this in northern Texas, where the garden was designed to have two watering systems: one for the roses and another for the boxwood hedge edging the garden. This was too much water for both the boxwood and the roses. In addition, the soil in the rose beds tended to be more clay-like and was retaining too much water, causing root rot. The solution here was to have just one watering system and reduce the amount and frequency of watering. The beds were also excavated and refinished with new soil that was a mix of organics and the native red sand-clay soil.

I've also experienced root rot on eastern Long Island (in New York) in a garden designed in a bowl-like landscape. Apparently at one time this was the site of a pond. The water table level was naturally high there, and every time the garden was irrigated or when it rained heavily, the water was actually standing around the roots in one area of the rose garden. As a result, the roots rotted, the plants died. The solution there was to excavate and put in a drain system and **refill the beds** with a sandy soil mix.

By mid-August I start allowing more hips to develop among the large shrub roses and climbers by deadheading less. By letting flowers just fade naturally on the shrub you will soon see hips swelling behind the faded petals. Species roses like *Rosa rugosa* will have a bounty of edible hips by now. This rose is also known as the "Tomato Rose" for good reason. If you've ever seen this rose growing wild all over the sand dunes along the coast, you can't miss the display of tomato-like rose hips. Another wonderful hip producer is the species *Rosa arkansana*. This North American native shows delicious-looking, shiny hips. Though not as big as the hips of *Rosa rugosa*, they are actually quite tasty!

Many cultivated varieties, such as 'Golden Wings', 'Complicata', 'New Dawn', and 'Inspiration', should begin showing hips now as well. These and many others will continue blooming as the hips form. I stop deadheading these larger shrubs now and allow hips to develop for a display that will last right through the winter (more on hips in **November**).

China and tea roses thrive in this weather, as my royalty display in pots will attest. 'Duchess of Kent', 'Duchesse de Brabant', and 'Archduke Charles' are finally starting to overflow the containers they're planted in with nodding blooms. With daily watering of the pots, I can almost see these roses growing right before my eyes, despite the heat.

*Rose hips come in various sizes and shapes.*

Your mulch will justify its existence during August, retaining moisture around the roots of the roses and, especially, keeping the roots cool. Try this test on a very hot day: Dig into the mulch with your hand and feel the soil underneath. It should be considerably cooler and moist. This is the job of the mulch, greatly improving the performance of your garden roses. Keep fluffing your mulch—this always looks nicer. But more important, it allows water and fertilizer to have quicker access to the root system.

Northern gardeners should take note that this will be the last month for fertilizing with a granular fertilizer and foliar feeding. This applies to any one in the regions that will be experiencing a frost in September or October. Meanwhile, regardless of where you garden, continue adding organic supplements to your soil.

I hear of all sorts of remedies for pest problems in the rose garden. Unfortunately many of those used freely by home gardeners are quite toxic. But today there are safer alternatives more readily available, and they really should be considered and taken seriously.

One ancient remedy for sucking insects (aphids, stem girdlers) involves spraying garden plants with garlic extractions and juices from other onion family (Allium) members. Some old-time garden books even recommend spreading the waste from beer kegs as a solution to keeping insects at bay. One of my garden volunteers kept his private rose collection free of insects, claiming that the beer hops mulch he used was the reason.

These remedies derived from plant sources are not as far-fetched as they might seem, since long before the advent of chemical sprays for pest control the source for pesticides was plant materials.

In Gerard's *Herball*, written in 1597, two pyrethrums (a pyrethrum is a type of chrysanthemum) are described as having great medicinal value. There are many of these chrysanthemum family members used in gardens today as ornamental plants, but one in particular, *Chrysanthemum cinerariaefoliium* (common name 'Dalmatian Pyrethrum') is the main source of **pyrethrum**, a pesticide named for the plant from which it is derived. This compound is from the flower heads, and today there are also synthetic forms available known as pyrethroids. **Pyrethroids** are considered broad-spectrum pesticides, meaning that they area useful in controlling a wide range of pests, and are of relatively low toxicity to mammals. The 'Painted Daisy' and other pyrethrums would make wonderful additions to any rose garden as companion plants.

Another natural pesticide, **rotenone**, is from the root of tropical legumes belonging to the plant family know as Derris. Though not a garden plant, the tropical climber *Derris elliptica* was the original source of rotenone. Today most of our rotenone powder comes from plants harvested in Peru. There are many synthetic versions of this pesticide available today, covering a wide range of insect and mite problems. Rotenone should be used with caution, since it is toxic to mammals. However, it is biodegradable.

**Sabadilla** is another natural pesticide from a tropical plant. The seeds of a Venezuelan lily, *Schoenocaulon officinale*, are the original source of this broad-spectrum, relatively safe, pesticide.

**Neem oil** has recently been discovered by Westerners to be a powerful and safe pesticide *and* fungicide, the source of the oil being the seeds of the Neem tree, a native plant of Eastern India.

Neem oil is an extract from the seed of the neem tree, a common tree in India. Basically, neem affects insects in two fashions. First, it causes the insect to stop eating, and second, it can disrupt their hormonal balance, ultimately affecting their reproductive and growth cycles. Neem residue does not function as a contact poison and it should be applied at the earlier stages of the insect's life cycle. Because it has to be ingested, neem will not harm beneficial organisms, only the insects that feed on the foliage that has been sprayed. The best news about neem is that it is not a threat to the environment or us.

**Ryania** is another pesticide of plant origin that could be useful in fighting thrip infestations. It has been successful in combating citrus thrips, common in areas where citrus fruits are farmed. Ryania is derived from the ground-up stemwood of a South America shrub, *Ryania speciosa*.

Nicotine, in the form of dusts and liquid sprays, was popular as a control of many soft-bodied insects, including aphids. This compound is not safe to use and not recommended. It was extracted from the tobacco plant—usually the waste material from the manufacturing of cigarettes and cigars. But it makes me wonder: If I use some of the wonderful ornamental tobaccos (*Nicotiana*) as companion plantings, will they act as a natural repellent?

My own experience with companion planting as a natural form of pest control is, now, quite extensive. **Since leaving the botanic garden, this is the style of rose gardening I prefer—especially in my own garden in southern New Jersey.** I've seen a dramatic decline in aphid and spider mite populations when I've planted garlic cloves with potted roses. I've also had the same effect when it came to using marigolds as an edge planting for ever-blooming roses. However, the deer didn't seem to mind these bright annuals; they found it very easy to reach past them and devour the new rosebuds.

I also recommend underplanting, with perennials and annuals with finely cut silver-gray foliage. This is a great color to add to the summer border. This is especially true in August when many roses have lost foliage from the bottom (sometimes as much as 50 percent of the plant's foliage), giving them a naked-knees effect. Companion planting with *Artemesia* 'Powis Castle', *Centurea* 'Colchester White', many varieties of nepeta, as well as the spreading *Helichrysum petiolare* (Silver-leaved Licorice plant) give the rose garden an added touch of color, often softening the harshness of the stick shapes of many roses in the heat of August.

When I make choices on what to include in my rose garden, I also select companion plants with fragrance. I choose plants such as lavender, mint (kept in a pot!), rosemary, nicotiana, agastache—all with fragrant foliage and/or flowers. Ancient garden books recommend the planting of parsley, nasturtiums, and species marigolds as edging to a rose bed to ward off uninvited dinner guests. And alliums were noted to have systemic powers, sending natural repellents up through the roots of the roses.

There are unlimited choices; the only word of caution is not to choose anything that will steal nutrients from the roses (such as deep-rooted trees and shrubs), or inhibit air circulation. Not only will the additional fragrances, textures, and colors enhance the beauty of your garden, but low-growing annuals and perennials like alyssum and thyme can also add a bit of cooling shade to the root and bud union of your roses.

One recent remedy for deer that I wouldn't consider is hanging rags soaked in creosote in your garden (Mom had read this somewhere on her quest to rid her neighborhood of deer) I've finally gotten her to stop with the garlic powder. I couldn't imagine dealing with the fragrance of creosote! The colorful netting is so much safer and effective as long as she keeps up with this.

**Just because it's the end of the summer you can't drop your guard.** The deer are getting hungry as autumn and winter approaches. With all of the new growth from pruning, and with rose hips forming, there's lots of fresh food in your garden. All it takes is one night of leaving the netting off, or leaving the garden gate open and it's like turning on a neon sign that says, **DEER DELI, OPEN FOR BUSINESS!**

# RECOMMENDED READING

*Climbing Roses*. Stephen Scanniello and Tania Bayard. New York: Prentice Hall, 1994

*Rose Companions*. Stephen Scanniello. Nashville, TN: Cool Springs Press, 2005

*Diseases of Trees and Shrubs*. Wayne A. Sinclair, Howard H. Lyon, Warren T. Johnson. Ithaca, NY. Cornell University Press, 1987

*The Gardener's Bug Book*. Cynthia Westcott. NY: Doubleday & Company. 4th ed. 1973

*The Plant Doctor*. Cynthia Westcott, Ph.D. New York. Frederic A. Stokes Company. 1937.

*Natural Insect Control*. Warren Schultz, editor. Brooklyn, NY. Brooklyn Botanic Garden Handbook # 139. 1994.

# RECOMMENDED MEMBERSHIP

Houston Rose Society
  P. O. Box 22614
  Houston, Texas 77227
  **www.houstonrose.org**

# FOR INFORMATION REGARDING THE NATIONAL EARTH KIND CULTIVARS

EarthKind™ Rose Website:
  **http://aggie-horticulture.tamu.edu/earthkindrose/**

# SEPTEMBER

I first smelled the musk rose in September—*not* in the spring when the eglantines are blooming, as Shakespeare erroneously reports. It is perhaps one of the rarest roses in the collection, and this is the month when this rather lanky, spreading shrub with heavily scented blooms comes into its peak display. The parent, from which my plant was propagated, has been blooming since early August in North Carolina, where it's trained onto an arbor and overflows with fragrant white flowers. Mine is living up to its reputation for having exquisite fragrance, but since it's susceptible to winter damage from my cold winters and a favorite of the rabbits, some seasons I may have to get down on my hands and knees to enjoy it.

September offers a chance for individual roses to stand out. As the days become shorter, the evenings have an edge of coolness, bringing on strong growth and the second major flush of roses for the season. For some this is only a brief moment, lasting a week or two before frost arrives. But gardeners in warmer regions of our country can look forward to another couple of months of great roses.

Don't expect the lushness of June, with rosebushes loaded from top to bottom with blooms. Ever-blooming climbers should be showing a fairly decent number of roses, but not the quantities that were on display a few months ago. Meanwhile, the once-blooming ramblers and climbers are now trained into place, and some are already displaying beautiful hips.

Many of the hybrid teas have naked bottoms, but still put on a display. The hybrid tea shrubs are taller than they were in June, the majority of them now stiff and upright showing their blooms predominantly from the middle of the plant toward the top. 'Roundelay', 'Jadis', 'Bride's Dream', and 'Curly Pink' are particularly beautiful now. Others, such as 'Maid of Honour', 'Country Doctor', and 'Peaudouce' are showing a graceful autumn habit loaded with large blooms.

Although there may not be as many blooms as in the spring, the autumn blooms are unsurpassed in size, and the colors are vivid and more intense with richer tones and hues. **In addition to the enhancement of fragrances, these are reasons why I love September.** But on the practical side, I *really* like September because this is when I stop deadheading and fertilizing.

It's a pleasure not to have to spend worktime removing faded clusters from the floribundas, and the polyanthas are again back into a respectable condition of bloom and growth. Despite the summer heat of the last couple of months, the floribundas 'Iceberg', 'Simplicity', and 'Betty Prior' have continued to bloom daily since June. My 'Mlle. Cécile Brunner' and 'Perle d'Or' (both polyanthas) are sending up long-branched clusters of blooms, each cluster offering dozens of sweetheart roses.

If you garden in a cold climate, it's not wise to encourage excessive new growth at this time, since frost may be imminent. If the rose is encouraged to continue growing, sending up new shoots and blooms, its likelihood of surviving a severe winter is questionable. Roses need to build up hardiness, and the wood needs to mature. As days become colder, there is a slowdown in new growth, making the rose more fit for the winter months ahead. Fertilizing and deadheading at this time will only work against this natural process.

Find out when the first frost is expected and stop deadheading and fertilizing about a month and a half before its arrival. In the New York region it's easy to remember Labor Day as the day to put down your pruning shears, the first possible frost for this region of the country being around mid-October.

The leaves are the food factories of all plants. From here the sugars are stored in the canes, bud unions, crowns, and roots. It's important to keep as much foliage on the roses now as possible so that they can build up a winter reserve. This may be a challenge, since cool evenings, sunny days, and high humidity are perfect conditions for **powdery mildew**, a common fungal disease. Powdery mildew deforms the foliage, giving it a distracting white coating. The disease occurs in the spring as well as in the autumn.

Unlike black spot, powdery mildew doesn't require a continual wet period to germinate. Once the spores are transported by moisture from humidity, dew, rain, or your irrigation system, they're happier if the surface they're growing on remains dry. For this reason, regular daytime washing of the foliage will prove beneficial.

This infectious disease makes its first appearance in an unassuming display as crinkled foliage. However, it's not very long before the powdery

*Powdery mildew will cause the younger leaves to crinkle and turn white, as if dusted with baby powder.*

phase appears. In spring, the white powder-like substance covers the newer foliage of many ramblers, particularly 'Crimson Rambler' and 'Evangeline'. But by the autumn, it is easily spotted on the new red leaves of all roses. When it's really bad you'll see it coating the canes, too.

Mildew has its favored conditions, and it's easy to prevent the disease from happening or at least from becoming a rampant problem. I treat powdery mildew lightly at this time of the year, not doing too much apart from giving my roses a daily hosing when the conditions are right for the spread of this disease. I'm more concerned about it on my ramblers trained on arches, and those displayed on pillars and festoons. The pruning described in July, especially the instructions for thinning out all clutter, will help tremendously in preventing its spread. And I avoid planting roses too close together. With ramblers, removal of the old wood after flowering is an easy way of ridding your garden of the problem.

There are, again, numerous fungicides available for controlling this fungus. But when I do go with something stronger than water, it's a solution of baking soda and water.

I wouldn't be surprised if one day baking soda will be registered and officially recognized as a garden fungicide. The solution I use was developed by Cornell University for controlling foliage diseases of roses including black spot and powdery mildew. **Use 2 tablespoons of a light-weight horticultural oil, 1 tablespoon of baking soda, and 1 gallon of** water. Mix this together and spray both sides of the leaf surface with a very fine mist. Keep shaking the container as you spray, and it's best to spray in the evening or early morning. Spray every five days if you have a severe problem. Personally, I find that two applications will do the job. I spray at the first sign of crinkled foliage, but even at a late stage, when the leaves have turned white, it's still possible to control further spread of the disease.

Mildew is almost guaranteed if a rose is planted in a location with poor air circulation, or in an area with less than ideal light. The canes of climbers crowded under eaves, and of old roses planted too far into the corner of a walled garden, are most likely to become infected. In September, my 'Peace' roses become shaded by crab apples in the afternoon as the sun begins to set lower in the sky. As the autumn progresses, these roses steadily succumb to mildew.

Droughts will bring on mildew. The spores are still capable of moving around in the moisture on humid evenings, and if there isn't much rain to wash the foliage, or if you're restricted from watering, they will thrive and proliferate, undeterred. Likewise, when it rains in the evening, or the roses go into the evening with wet foliage, you can almost see mildew appear right before your eyes.

If your roses continue to be mildew-prone, follow through with a weekly spray program for as long as the weather stays cool and the conditions are right. I ignore my mildew problems now, since it won't be too long before the leaves start to fall, anyway. I'm concerned about it when it appears in the spring. However, in warmer regions of the country, where there's no danger of frost until January, if at all, an easy way of dealing with autumn mildew and other foliage pests is to reprune your roses. In warm climate areas of our country, September's cooler weather signals the end of the summer dormancy, and you should begin pruning now to encourage the best autumn blooms.

Throughout these regions, the roses that are going to look best with the least amount of work will be the China and tea roses. But there is also a wide palette of modern hybrids, especially those having a stronger heritage of these antique roses in their blood.

I like most hybrid teas, but I find myself favoring those introduced from the late 1800's through the first two decades of the twentieth century. On a recent Labor Day visit to the E.M. Mills Rose Garden in Syracuse, New York, one of the oldest public rose garden in the United States, an original planting of 'Lady Ursula' (hybrid tea, 1908) filled one bed with hundreds of nodding pink flowers on plants with lush green foliage. In my opinion, none of the modern hybrids could hold a candle to her.

Hybrid tea roses like 'Lady Ursula' were the pioneers of their class, exhibiting more of a tea rose influence than those of today. In fact, many of these early hybrids were indeed true hybrids of tea roses. Many are still grown today and are quite easy to find. Other beauties to search for would be 'La France', 'Mme. Caroline Testout', 'Mme. Jules Bouché', and 'Mrs. Arthur Robert Waddell'. In the cool late summer weather and early autumn sunlight, their soft colors and lush foliage make the September rose garden a real joy.

Speaking of searching, this is the last month to put together an order for bare-rooted roses to be planted this year. The sooner you can order them, the better. With roses it's very true that "the early bird gets the worm." The few nurseries that ship bare root roses in the autumn have deadlines for accepting orders. **Potted roses have a longer shipping period and you can plant these as long as the ground isn't frozen.** If you plan on adding roses to your garden this year, or if you want to spend more time planning for the spring, this would be a good time to consider a new rose bed.

Rose beds can be any shape you wish. What's important is that you don't make them too wide or too large to handle. Design your beds so that you can easily perform chores such as deadheading, weeding, and fertilizing from the surrounding paths and borders. Walking in among the roses is hazardous to their health. Heed the warning of the prickles, and stay out of the rose beds whenever possible.

The *only* time I enter a rose bed is for pruning and planting. Even then, I make sure that I stay in one place as much as possible and limit the amount of stepping I do in the planted areas.

Deadheading is probably the most difficult job to do when the roses are out of reach. I have seen too many flowers broken off before they can ever open when someone moves freely through the rose bed to deadhead.

To make your work as easy as possible, an ideal bed would be from $3^1/2$ to 5 feet wide. Of course, if you have a long reach, you can go wider. Design the bed so that you can get to it from all sides. Otherwise you can create a narrow pathway, either entirely through the bed, or at least until you've reached a spot where you can comfortably reach the roses you can't get at from the side.

**It's always important to be sensitive to every step you make in a rose bed.**

There are good reasons for this, the obvious one being that branches will break off, sometimes very easily, when brushed against. You not only create safe harbor for pests whenever you break off a piece of new growth, you can also transport insect eggs, adults of non-flying pests (aphids, mites), and move fungi spores around the garden when you step out of one bed and into another.

Stepping into the beds will damage feeder roots located just a few inches below the surface. And it causes compaction, limiting the amount of air and water in the soil and thereby inhibiting root growth.

Variations on rectangular or square patterns are typical of many rose beds. A traditional formal design is a large circular bed divided into four wedge-shaped parterre beds. Each bed is separated by a 2-foot-wide path and edged in boxwood. In the center is a smaller circular bed, planted with a climber trained up a pillar or obelisk.

A favorite design of mine is a bed shaped sort of like a paisley or a kidney. Every curve of the bed allows me access into the center areas without having to step in. If I have a series of these, I like to add a repeating feature of pillars, and maybe even connect the beds with simple arches.

Another more formal idea would be to create a half-circular bed, let's say with a straight side about 25 feet long, along a walkway. If you stand at midpoint, the depth of the bed would be about 12½ feet from the walkway to the farthest point on the curve. This is too deep for working in without stepping in among the roses. To remedy this problem, run a path through the bed, following the shape of the curve. Start from the walkway at one end of the bed and come back out to the walkway at the other end. If you make the path just wide enough for one person to walk through the bed with a bucket for cutting rose or deadheading, it will make the entire planting area accessible.

To make the garden more interesting, place a pillar or a tripod at either end of the bed to display climbing roses. If you have room, you can expand the design by creating another bed facing this one, on the opposite side of the walkway. Even separated from each other by a path as wide as 8 feet, you can still connect them with an arch from pillar to pillar.

One very effective way of adding a bed of roses into a very small space would be to have a circular bed with a tripod or pillar underplanted with rosebushes. Make the bed a diameter of 6 feet. Centered in this bed could be a tripod, or a pyramidal structure, as wide as 3 feet at the base and up to 10 feet high.

On this structure you can plant up to three climbers if it's a tripod, four roses on a pyramid, or one climber or tall growing shrub on a single pillar. Depending on how many climbers or what sort of structure you decide on, you could add up to ten hybrid teas or moderate-sized shrubs into a bed of this design.

As you can imagine, the styles and variations are endless. Here are some guidelines to consider when estimating the appropriate number of plants per bed.

Plant as close as 2 feet from the edge of the bed for large shrubs, 6 inches from the edge if you're using the smallest varieties of miniatures ('Cinderella', for example), and one foot from the edge with polyantha roses. This will result in a slight spillover of color into the pathways, creating a more natural and less formal look. Make alterations on this spacing if you want to create an edging of another type of plant.

Instead of planting rosebushes in straight lines with the bed like wooden soldiers, stagger the plantings. Be creative in how you group your roses.

One way to make hybrid teas more attractive as garden shrubs is to plant three of more plants of a particular cultivar together. A traditional way to display ever-blooming roses is to plant several of the same cultivar in one bed. An alternative might be to plant clusters of three in a **V** formation, or fives in a **W**. Another method would be to plant the fives in an **X** pattern, with four corners and a center, like dots on the five side of a die. But the way to plant with the thought of making pest control a priority would be to interplant with other plants like annuals, perennials, and

*To make a dramatic display, plant the same cultivar in groups of three or five.*

herbs, and not to put two disease-prone types together. (Remember: The yellows are always suspect.)

Hybrid teas, floribundas, and grandifloras often look best when grouped in arrangements of three or five. Larger shrubs like the English roses create a wonderful display when planted in groups of three. The same applies for the old roses, while minis and polyanthas tend to look good in groups of three or five.

The larger the shrub, the more space should be allowed between plants. Minis and polyanthas can be as close as 1 foot apart. Hybrid teas do best from 2$\frac{1}{2}$ to 3 feet apart. Shrub roses (old and new) should be at least 3 feet apart but look the best when spaced 4 to 5 feet, and climbers and wide-spreading shrubs should be spaced no close than 6 feet apart.

In searching for a site for a rose bed, be aware of the path of the sun and any nearby trees., especially those with invasive roots. Roses prefer a southern exposure and need at least five hours of sun for their best performance. But even a north slope or the north side of a building will work so long as there is sufficient sunlight. Whenever possible, consider the value of some shade in your garden. Afternoon shade in particular can be a relief to the roses, at times creating more intense colors and stronger fragrances compared to roses growing in full sun.

Try not to plan your bed in a low area, or bowl, in the landscape. The drainage is going to be poor here, and cold air collects in low spots, putting the roses in danger of exposure to both early and late frosts.

Roses near the ocean and saltwater bays can suffer salt spray damage or worse from winds and flooding, while mildew problems will be increased due to cool evening dampness in the air. Then there's the added threat of damage from icy winter winds coming off the waters.

Hedges, fencing, and walls can be built to amend these problems and at the same time add beauty to your rose garden. However, make sure that you continue to have good air circulation around the roses at all times if you build any sort of windbreak.

If you are in a warm climate, watch for **nematodes** in the soil. There are many types of nematodes, though not all are bad. Over-irrigated, warm sandy soils are ideal for a nematode infestation. If there was an old garden previously in the spot you're thinking of using for your new planting, and there was a nematode problem with the prior garden, chances are that the nematodes will still be there, and that's not good. It's also very likely that you can bring in a nematode population with the root ball of an infected plant.

Nematodes are microscopic worms that get into the roots of plants and feed on them. They disrupt the growing habits of roses often resulting in tip dieback, root rot, yellowing leaves, and stunted growth. I experienced this pest while working on a garden in Texas. Nematodes were invading the rose beds as a result of over-irrigation and over-fertilizing of the boxwood hedge that served as a border for the beds. In the autumn, a distinct reddish cast to the foliage of the boxwood and the rotting roots were pretty good indications that there was a nematode problem. Eventually, the boxwoods were removed, and all of the soil replaced.

The best thing to do if you're not sure whether you have nematodes or not is to send a sample of soil *and* roots to your local horticulture extension agent for testing.

If you have nematodes, they're difficult to get rid of. One solution is to stop growing roses on the site for several years, or, change all of your soil, excavating beyond the area where you are growing roses. Of course, if you're going to go through all of this trouble, make sure you've corrected any situations that may encourage the spread of nematodes. **Make the necessary adjustments to your fertilizing and irrigation schedules.**

Plant-damaging nematodes are more common in warmer regions and not common at all in cold climates. If you live in a warm climate, check with our local rose society about nematode problems. **Purchase your roses from a reputable nursery, one that knows the best rootstock for your region.** Nematodes need warm, moist soil to reproduce, so don't create this environment in your garden. Evaluate your water system. Flooding of the beds can also move the nematodes around, spreading the problem. Increase the organic content of your soil to encourage more beneficial insects—there are many that will prey on nematodes.

A final word of caution on selecting a site for a new rose bed: Have there been any roses recently growing on this site? If so, for how long? Perhaps you've heard or read about a mysterious phenomenon referred to as **rose soil sickness**. Something in the soil, left behind by older rose bushes, seems to have a negative affect on the growth of newly planted roses when these roses have been planted in exactly the same location as the old ones. In England and France, it's common practice to replant rose beds in public gardens every seven years with a complete replacement of the soil.

I believe this problem exists, but I don't know of any explanation for its occurrence. No one has been able to scientifically prove if there is an actual poison exuded from the roots of the old rose roots, or if it has something to do with the rootstocks used. There are lots of theories to study an compare, especially if you do a search online for "rose soil sickness." From my experiences, rose soil sickness doesn't happen all of the time in our gardens, but it's a worthwhile concern to be aware of.

I don't recommend digging up your garden every seven years. But be aware of the possibility of soil sickness when you are going to plant a new rose bush in a spot where an older bush had been growing for a very long time. In this situation, I would recommend changing the soil in the immediate area where the older plant was growing. Otherwise, as long as your roses are flourishing, leave them be. Roses can live for a very long time in one location.

In September, artists who frequent the rose gardens are attracted to the festoons in the hybrid tea beds. The festoons, or swags, are created by training ramblers onto chains hanging over the rose beds. By September, the chains become overgrown, with long whips spilling down into the roses below. I suppose that to the artists this chaotic style is romantic and inspiring. It's inspiring to me, too, but for different reasons. I'm inspired to start pruning again, to train the canes further along the chains, and to save the roses below from being overcrowded.

Festoons are absolutely stunning in the early summer when they area covered in blooms. In September they're a challenge.

To create a festoon, the rose canes are wrapped around a narrow, hanging support such as a chain, a wire, or rope. I have 10-feet-high posts set

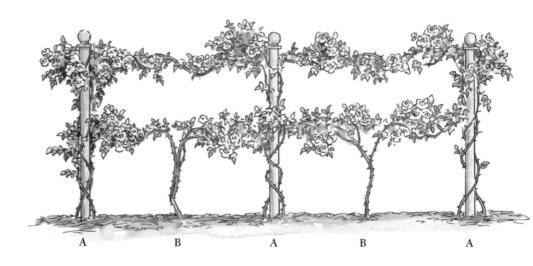

A B A B A

*A double-layer festoon is created by planting ramblers at the base of the pillars (A), training their canes up to the top chains, and planting ramblers at the midpoints (B), training them onto the lower chains.*

A YEAR OF ROSES

12 feet apart. The material that creates the festoon is a 1-inch-link chain strung in a graceful curve from post to post. Among my most successful festoons is one trained with 'Albéric Barbier', a white French rambler. In two years' time I trained four canes up onto the chain and eventually covered it along its entire length.

I prefer to use the French ramblers created at the beginning of the twentieth century by M. Barbier of Paris. Most of these were bred using a tea rose as a parent, resulting in wonderful bursts of growth in the autumn. Not only do you have the flexible canes and lush growth, you also have tea rose-like blooms in the early summer. The effect is magical: a garland of roses when in bloom, followed by a swag of lush foliage, and sometimes, even hips.

The actual training of the roses into a festoon is very similar to the technique used for creating an arch: Keep just enough canes to cover the required distance. The rest are pruned off of the festoon (at great disappointments to the artists). Keep the longest canes and wrap them around the chain as tightly as you possibly can. Three canes will produce a full garland of blooms next season.

**Throughout the gardening season it will be necessary to prune away any short canes that can't make it up onto the chain.** These will only crowd out other roses planted around the base of the pillar.

There are several variations of this design. The most common way to create a festoon is to run a swag from the top of one post to another. Another design would be to swag the chain almost to the ground and plant the rose at the low point of the curve, training the canes upward toward the posts. There's a beautiful display of the climber 'American Pillar' trained in this fashion in the rose garden at Loose Park in Kansas City, Missouri.

If you have a series of arches, one after another, you can create festoons of roses along the sides, connecting the arches and making them into a pergola. Run straight supports from one arch to another, at least from peak to peak, and maybe add two more parallel pieces on either side of the center. This will give your ramblers and climbers more room for their rampant canes. More important, you will now have a fragrant entrance into your garden.

Ever-blooming climbers are more difficult to use in this manner, because of their stiff growth habit. And I painfully learned that not all ramblers are as flexible as you might wish. I have 'Bobbie James', a white rambler from England, trained as a festoon. More than the flowers, I love the hips. They look beautiful all winter long hanging off the chain. But when the hooked prickles dig into my arms every time I attempt to tame this beast, I wonder what ever possessed me to use 'Bobbie James' in such a detailed position.

The thick, nearly woody canes don't want to twist, and I'm afraid that the weight of the old wood might even pull down the pillars supporting the chains. There's a good chance that in November I'll end up transplanting the fast-growing rambler to a fence.

**An update on 'Bobbie James': I never had a chance to move the plant, but the year after I left the garden, the new rosarian banished this English beast to the hillside.**

Sometimes a climber will create its own festoon, whether you planned it or not. In my mom's garden in southern New Jersey we planted several climbers along her driveway using the supports for her carport as pillars. By the end of the second year, the climbers had reached the top of their columns and spread out into a neighbor's driveway (to their displeasure!). After dropping several hints of how much she would love a chain to run from pillar to pillar, Mom went ahead and took the canes of 'New Dawn' and designed her own festoon by weaving canes from 'New Dawn' together with those from the climber on the next pillar, 'Dortmund'. The neighbors are, once again, tolerant of Mom's roses.

Mom has had great luck in the war against the deer, but not so with Mother Nature. **During a major snowstorm in 2004, the carport collapsed.** The only casualties were the roses—all of the canes were broken to the ground. Two years later, we're now back to coaxing new canes up onto the supports of the new carport, and of course, with colorful netting! Next year she'll have swags again.

---

## RECOMMENDED READING
*Easy Care Roses.* Stephen Scanniello. Editor. Brooklyn, NY: Brooklyn Botanic Garden, 1995

## RECOMMENDED FOR MORE INFORMATION ON ORGANIC CONTROLS:
- The website of the Santa Clarita Valley Rose Society: http://www.scvrs.homestead.com
- An interesting forum dealing with organic solutions: Global Healing Center. http://www.ghchealth.com/forum/organic-garden-helps-amp-solutions-discussion

## RECOMMENDED MEMBERSHIP
Johnson County Rose Society: www.rosesocietyjoco.org
Serves the Kansas City area

# OCTOBER

Heavy morning dews and scatterings of frost have left some of the white roses tinged pink, the pink roses looking redder, and the apricots golden. This is typical of an October morning in the rose garden.

The plum-colored canes of *Rosa setigera* are a perfect foil for the now intense orange-red leaves of this North American native. *Rosa arkansana, Rosa carolina,* and *Rosa virginiana* all add to the display with their wonderful fire-orange colors, while at the same time putting on a vibrant hip display. The show is not limited to the species roes. There are many old roses such as 'Duc de Guiche', 'La Belle Sultane', and 'Alain Blanchard' that have attractive foliar color in the autumn. On the other hand, as the season progresses, hybrid teas, floribundas, and many of the shrub roses are again living up to their reputation as resembling gangly sticks poking out of the mulch, but still in bloom. Densely petaled hybrids like 'Fair Bianca' and 'Uncle Joe' stay tightly shut, while other hybrids such as 'Dainty Bess', 'Monsieur Tillier', and 'Autumn Sunset' are bursting with color and fragrance.

Among the roses still blooming, the ones I especially enjoy in October are growing in large stone pots at the top of the steps to the rose pavilion. In each 15-inch pot with a decorative lattice motif, there is a single tea rose. By October, these colorful accents to the garden with their opulence of bloom, are hard to miss. The tea roses I grow directly in the ground are beautiful, too, but in my climate they rarely reach a comfortable viewing height. I usually end up crawling around to look up into their nodding blooms. These, displayed in their pots, give me the opportunity to enjoy their prolific October blooms without getting my knees wet. My first personal rose garden was an old wooden tub I inherited with a second-floor Brooklyn apartment. Sitting on the top step of our stoop, this old planter was barely held together by a few rusty nails. I knew if I moved it, I would lose all the soil, because the bottom was not quite in line with the rest of the container. But it did have good drainage!

The stoop was the sunniest part of the front "yard," so I planted the container (18 inches wide by 18 inches tall) with sun lovers. I had a mum for autumn color, a few volunteer petunia seedlings from a previous owner, a gorgeous moonflower vine that twined its way up to our kitchen window, and four miniature roses: 'Winter Magic', 'Simplex', 'Trinket', and 'Orchid Jubilee'. I didn't have any special reason for selecting these cultivars; they just happened to be orphans from the botanic garden collection.

It was a bit crowded, but every now and then, with very little effort, I had a few roses on my front stoop that I could call my own.

Not everyone has a space to grow roses in the ground. But maybe on the deck, the front stoop, or outside a sunny window, there's a space for at least one flowerpot or window box. You can create a satisfactory rose garden in containers. Any rose, from the tiniest miniature to the most vigorous climber, will grow and bloom in a container garden.

Container gardening is popular in the city, and strolling through my Brooklyn neighborhood I see different styles of containers on display, adding color to the fronts of the working-class row houses. There are wooden tubs, fancy terra-cotta (usually chained to the railings), cement troughs, and even dilapidated antique wheelbarrows overflowing with all sorts of plantings, and almost always with at least one rose.

Traveling around the country, I find the most interesting planters are the ones made from household items, and from stuff that you would find in the back of the garage or under the cellar stairs.

Cinder blocks and chimney flues overflow with miniature roses, as do wooden and plastic dairy crates, the ubiquitous inverted truck-tire sculpture—three tires high, and red, white, and blue, with scalloped edges at the top—and my favorite: a bathtub with claw feet, planted with petunias and a rose climbing the fan trellis. The finishing touch in many of these gardens is a statue of the Virgin standing guard nearby.

Put your container on wheels and you can take your garden with you. Move your garden to where the sun is, or bring the garden to your side if you desire to sit in the shade and enjoy the fragrance of fresh roses at the same time. Wheels will also make it easier when you need to corral the pots together for winter protection.

Putting a rose bush into a pot doesn't change the growing needs of a rose. They still need rich, organically loaded potting soil, lots of sunshine, and, most important, water. If anything should change because of their

A YEAR OF ROSES

being in a container, it's the watering: You'll have to check more often to see if this rose needs water.

When you grow a rose in a pot or a box, all sides, as well as the top of the pot, are exposed to the weather. On very hot days, water will be lost a great deal faster from the container than if the rose were growing in the ground. Similar logic applies to winter protection. Since the root system is exposed from the sides of the pot, you should remember to create some sort of insulating layer along the sides of the container if it is exposed to winter winds.

Whatever container you use should be big enough to support the root system of the rose and have drainage holes in the bottom. Don't waste time or money with a pot that doesn't have at least four 1-inch drainage holes.

Regular applications of water-soluble fertilizer are important, but don't overdo it. Fertilizers can cause a salt buildup in the container, very

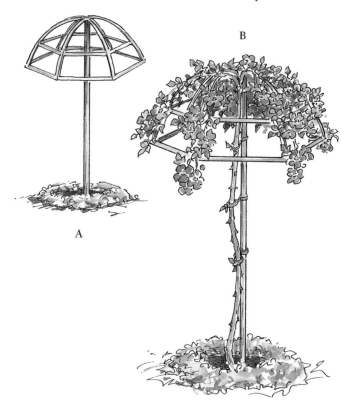

*Weeping standards are much more interesting than the typical lollipop styles. Umbrella structures (A) are used to train the canes of standard forms of climbers or shrub roses to give them a controlled look (B).*

damaging to the root system. I use liquid fertilizer every two weeks, but at half the rate recommended on the package. Also, in the beginning of the season add a small amount of slow-release fertilizer to the soil mix. In a pot 2-feet-wide and 2-feet-deep I add about 2 tablespoonfuls.

**Don't be stingy with the size of the container.** Get a container that will allow the roots lots of room to grow. Yellow leaves with a container-grown rose bush usually indicate that the container is too small for the plant or the roses had become root bound. This happens often with miniature roses.

Miniature roses arrive from the nursery in little plastic pots that are just barely big enough to hold the rose. If the mini is left in one of these small pots, it won't be long before leaves start turning yellow and dropping off. Upgrade the mini to at least a 4-inch pot as soon as possible.

At the local nursery, larger rose types like hybrid teas, climbers, shrubs, and old garden roses are usually potted into 10-inch plastic pots. If you left the rose in this pot, it would survive as long as you watered it daily and gave it ample sunshine. However, compare a potted rose to another of the same variety in a bigger pot or in the ground. You'll see the difference a larger root space can make.

Container gardening is the only way to grow roses on the top of a tall building or on a terrace. I've successfully grown climbers on rooftops of apartment buildings in New York, some as high as thirteen stories above midtown Manhattan. My favorite containers for this are round tubs cut from pickle or whiskey barrels, or long wooden boxes, at least 18 inches wide and 2 feet deep.

In a 2-feet-wide container (square or round), I plant one climber or one large shrub. There is enough room to plant up to five miniature roses. Polyanthas and small Chinas can be planted in groups of threes. Minis and polyanthas also can be used to underplant larger shrub roses in the same container.

Tree roses, also called standard roses, are often displayed to their best advantage when planted in containers. In my opinion, this is the best way to use these whimsical novelties created for decorating gardens. Any rose cultivar can be used to create a tree rose. Tree roses come in heights anywhere from 2 feet high (most common with miniature roses) to over 6 feet.

There are two forms of standard roses available. One is the common form of a long stem supporting a bushy display of roses, sort of like a large lollipop. The other is a weeping standard, the only style I think worth using.

Tree roses are created by attaching three buds of a rose cultivar to a long straight stem of another rose. The two most commonly used as stem stock are 'Dr. Huey' and an unnamed rugosa rose variety. Other roses have been used for creating standards, but the rugosa seems to be the strongest, surviving the longest.

Buds are grafted onto this straight stem and then are trained to grow just as if they were regular rose shrubs on the ground level. The majority of the lollipop tree roses are made from popular hybrid teas, floribundas, grandiflora, and miniature roses. Of all of these, the floribundas are the best looking. But if I were using a tree rose, I would only want a weeping tree rose.

Weeping tree roses are created in the same fashion as the bushy types, except that the buds used are climbing roses (ramblers, most of the time), ground cover roses, and even larger shrub roses. These are much more interesting because of the wonderful cascading effect they create in the garden. Most of the roses used are going to have a natural arching cane habit, giving you that weeping form without you having to do much work. Sometimes, however, you have to help the canes grow downward by training them to a structure such as an umbrella hoop, or by tying fishing sinkers to the canes. (Experiment with the weights; I've used 2-ounce lead sinkers.)

One of the best weeping tree roses I ever saw was in an amateur rose grower's garden in Kansas City, Missouri. At the top of a 6-foot stem of 'Dr. Huey', this rosarian budded several buds of the miniature climbing rose 'Red Cascade'. The fountain of red roses in his June garden display was one of the most spectacular sites I've ever seen.

I spotted another tree rose I liked while driving west on the interstate from the city of Shreveport, Louisiana on the way to the airport. Out of the corner of my eye I could see this massive display of large white roses hanging off a tree-like stem that had to be about 6 feet tall. It was in a nursery yard, and I had no idea what rose it was, except that it was beautiful. If I had been driving back to Brooklyn, I would have taken it with me.

Miniatures, small polyanthas, and small China roses can be used to edge large boxes, especially under tree roses.

Miniature roses are ideal for window boxes. One 24-inch box can comfortably hold four rosebushes. There are some miniature roses that are praised as cascading types, but I've found that many aren't as delicate looking as they might sound. They're actually better suited as ground cover roses (see **November**) or even for growing onto pillars. If you want a cascading effect over the edges of pots, try annuals such as alyssum or lobelia. There are also many cultivars of thyme that can add a soft texture to containers and are especially beautiful with roses.

Another gardening technique that doesn't take up a large amount of space, and adds an interesting vertical element, is growing roses on pillars.

*A tight fit, but full look, would be to plant two climbers per pillar (A). I've used two pillars leaning toward each other (B) and intertwined the climbers to create a sort of false tripod.*

With a pillar rose you direct as much of the growth upward as you possibly can, tying the canes in close to any upright structure instead of letting the rose spill into your garden.

A pillar can be as simple as a single cedar post, or a more complex design such as a circular or square metal design. Some of these are capped with umbrella-type hoops for training the canes of any rose into a weeping rose effect. Pillars can be added to a garden to serve as corner markers or to draw attention to the center of a flowerbed. Several in a line will create a backdrop to a garden, or they can simply be set alone, becoming the focus of the garden.

Look around in your garden. I'm sure there is something there that you can use to train a rose or two up onto. Porch columns, supports for the carport, post lanterns: These are all possibilities. How about the laundry line post?

While visiting the private rose garden of David and Helga Dawn in Southampton, New York, I was in awe of their spectacular display of pillar roses. At close inspection I discovered the simple technique David used to create his eight-foot pillars. When the roses were planted, five-foot iron snow fence supports were put into position alongside the plant. The thin but heavy bar was planted 2 feet deep. As the rosebush outgrew this post, a new one was simply bolted onto the old, increasing its height. As the shrub or climber matured, the canes were twined around and around the iron post. Eventually, the post was completely hidden from sight by the dense growth and blooms of the rosebush.

When I use wood, I prefer my pillars to be round, 6 inches in diameter. If you don't have a post in your garden ready for a rose, you can plant a rose and the pillar at the same time, with the pillar anchored 2 feet into the ground. As the rose grows, wrap the canes around the pillar, starting about 1 foot from the ground level. When wrapping more than one cane, run them parallel to each other, stretching them upward, to get the most coverage on the pillar. Eventually, the canes will reach beyond the pillar creating a "fountain" look. But at some point you'll have to shorten these canes. Otherwise they'll just whip around in the wind.

Some roses have canes that wrap easily, while others are not so compliant. Adding crosspieces or even just large nails to the pillars will give you something to attach string to. This prevents the canes from bunching together on the column. Cedar posts with the remains of the old branches on them are perfect pillars.

Eventually, after a few seasons, there will be more canes than you can use. One solution to this is to allow some of the canes to create a "skirt" around the base of the pillar. 'Frau Karl Druschki', 'La Belle Sultane', and 'Mme. Hardy' are naturals for this technique. Keep the longest canes for training onto the structure and shorten the rest to various lengths, allowing them to hang at different levels and lengths around the base of the post. It will require more room than just an ordinary pillar, but this enables you to use more of the rose instead of pruning severely to make it fit your garden. The effect is magical: a pillar of roses emerging from a mound of color.

Pillars are an easy addition to any garden, and suitable for antique hybrids as well as for numerous modern-day shrubs and climbers. Try not to use climbers with exceptional vigor, such as 'Mermaid' and 'Inspiration'. Instead, consider selecting from three old rose groups: hybrid Chinas, hybrid Bourbons, and hybrid Noisettes. I have found that the best way to show off the large fragrant flowers of these spring-bloomers is to train them as pillar roses.

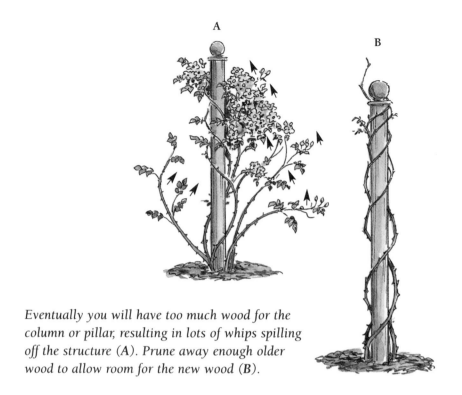

*Eventually you will have too much wood for the column or pillar, resulting in lots of whips spilling off the structure (A). Prune away enough older wood to allow room for the new wood (B).*

These rose groups date from the nineteenth century, having arrived as offshoots and culls in the quest to create ever-blooming climbing roses. They evolved from a very mixed heritage of European old garden roses that were hybridized with China, Noisette, and Bourbon roses. This "lost generation" had a relatively short heyday, most commonly used during the nineteenth century with their long canes tied to decorative Victorian pillars. The French discovered that the more the canes were manipulated, the larger the crop of blooms, their weight often pulling the canes down to the ground.

Over the decades, as cold-hardy ever-blooming roses became a reality, these classes were dropped from catalogs (though not all of the roses were). Only a handful of the original varieties survive today, and they have been absorbed into other rose classes such as gallicas, albas, and centifolia roses. But there is a movement today among dedicated rosarians and nursery people to bring back the old system of classifying hybrid China, hybrid Noisette, and hybrid Bourbon.

Minimal pruning is the trick with these roses. The more they are pruned, the less they will bloom. Remove deadwood, unclutter criss-crossing branches and shorten each lateral—that is any branch that is untrainable or shorter than your arm's length. That's all.

As you train your roses up onto pillars and start cleaning up debris from the beds, you might notice clusters of bright orange spots appearing on the undersides of leaves and sometimes on deadwood. In October, with frequent morning dews and temperatures hovering in the mid-50, it's the perfect environment for the development of **rust**. Yes, yet another fungal disease!

Rust is not widespread nationally, or at least not in the epidemic proportions that black spot and mildew are. This fungus has been found in all the Eastern coastal states and as far west as the Rockies. But it's in coastal California and along the entire Pacific Northwest coast where rust is a problem. Rust does best where there are mild winters, cool temperatures, and long periods of moisture from excessive rain, heavy dew mornings, and fog. If a leaf is wet for at least four hours, and the temperature is below eighty degrees, then you have ideal conditions for rust.

You could have had rust, and never may have noticed it. Or, you could be mistaking other problems for rust. My experience with this fungus is that I only see it on plant parts that are close to water faucets with a continual leak. I've also come across it in gardens very near the seashore. Sometimes, reddish discoloration on foliage due to spray damage or cold weather, or even some obscure leaf spot diseases can be mistaken for rust. But the genuine article is very distinctive in its appearance.

At its most noticeable stage, rust appears as clusters of little dots of orange on the underside of foliage. This causes discoloration of the leaves leading to defoliation. If you are in a rust-prone region, it's absolutely essential that you clear your garden in autumn and winter of infected and fallen foliage, as well as all dead canes. Rust over-winters as black pustules in garden debris. This phase is not as detectable as the rust-colored stage. Winter sprays of lime-sulfur will help control the problem.

Did you have a severe aphid problem this year? If so, now is the time to do something about them. In the cool autumn weather, the males and females are getting back together to produce the eggs that overwinter for the spring outbreak. Destroy as many of the aphids as possible with a blast of water oil sprays, or insecticidal soap.

October is the month I start planting spring flowering bulbs. I try to plan on having bulbs in bloom while the roses are dormant; while the roses are in their full flush of bloom; and during the summer when the roses go into their rest mode. For an early spring display I use chionodoxa and puschkinia—both naturalize beautifully through the garden, coming into bloom just as I finish my spring rose pruning. Next come the multitudes of narcissus, from the earliest jonquils to the large classic yellow varieties. The season of daffodils for me ranges from late March thru the middle of May, ending just as the old garden roses are coming into their first glimpse of color.

Tulips join the spring display as the daffodils are beginning to wane and the old garden roses are coming into a serious bloom. From antique species to the most modern cottage tulips, these are fun bulbs to mix in with roses. The latest blooming tulips, Darwins and Late Season varieties, usually are just peaking as the first flower buds of my China rose, 'Sophie's Perpetual' and the buds of 'Marie Pavié' are showing color.

The early summer season of bulbs coincides beautifully with the first flush of roses—old and modern. As the roses are beginning to take center stage, the alliums and camassia add cool colors to the garden. The classic globe-type alliums (Globemaster, Gladiator, Mt. Everest) stand out high above hybrid teas and other shrub types. *Allium christophii*, a looser form of the globe allium, pokes out from below the roses. Unlike its taller cousins, this allium only reaches a height of 18 inches.

Camassia, a native bulb with varieties in different shades of blue and white, looks great around the "skirts" of the old garden roses.

As the first flush of roses comes to an end, the lilies begin putting on their show. These perennials naturalize well in the garden and you can extend the season of bloom from late spring through to late summer with the numerous varieties of antique and modern hybrids. I find that tall growing tiger lilies emerging through the delicate foliage of shrub roses such as *Rosa primula* or 'Harison's Yellow' are an exquisite site. Plant the bulbs within the canopy of the shrub rose; these lilies will find their way through the foliage, coming into bloom in mid-summer as the roses begin their summer dormancy.

Walking through the October garden I notice a problem far worse than rust, aphids, or any sucking insects. Rabbits have been feeding on my roses, fattening up for the winter on a diet of new rose leaves and succulent new canes. They seem to have a keen sense of where my favorite roses are. I have yet to see the 'Tipsy Imperial Concubine' in bloom or several of my Bermuda beauties. Just as soon as a flower bud develops, it's gone—with the perfect slice of rabbit teeth. These roses must be a delicacy for rabbits: They'll pass up 'Betty Prior' any day for a taste of "Bermuda's Kathleen".

Apart from offering variations on hasenpfeffer, my humane solution is to spray the roses with an animal repellent. The chemicals are effective and safe. You simply spray the foliage of roses that continually get eaten. Once the critters get a taste, they stay away from anything that has been sprayed. Sometimes one warning is all it takes, and no harm is done to the animals.

But as October comes to an end, I notice that my winter garden sentinel has returned: a large red-tailed hawk with a big appetite.

# November

Rosarians are crazy. And I've learned that the New Yorkers among them can be the craziest. As the summer-long drought is finally coming to an end with blinding rain, bolts of lightning, and cold winds whipping through the rose pavilion, two dozen rosarians have been lined up outside the garden gates of the Cranford Rose Garden, all waiting for their chance to dig up a rosebush and transplant it to their own garden. Noticing their studied ragtag and peasant-chic garden gear, and a very odd collection of spading implements, I can't help wondering if the mad doctor has been up to something funny again at some nearby castle.

It's the final phase of a massive soil replacement project. The last three rose beds will be completely excavated in preparation for a new high organic soil mix to give the rose collection a long-needed boost. Many of the faces outside the gate I recognize from previous rose digs, or perhaps I saw them in the garden making notes on which rose they were going to dig on this first Saturday of November. They're not really so crazy; they know that November is a very good month to plant and transplant roses.

You can plant a rose anytime, as long as there isn't a imminent threat of severe cold or hot weather. Transplanting is planting; the only difference is that you're moving a rose deeply rooted in your own, or someone else's garden, from one place to another.

Transplanting is easy. You can move a rose of just about any size or age, with no long-term damaging effects. In fact, transplanting will often restore the vigor of an old rosebush. I view transplanting as the chance to give the plants, and you, a new start in the garden.

Moving an old rosebush also gives you the rare opportunity to see what's going on underground. Take a careful look at the root system, checking for problems such as root rot, gall, and rootstock suckering. Root rot is suspect if you detect a foul odor from the soil as you dig. The cauliflower-like shapes of gall should be easy to spot when the roots are exposed. And you'll actually see the suckers originating from the rootstock if you are moving a budded rose.

There are lots of treasures to be found. Perhaps you'll uncover an old nursery tag, finally giving away the secret of grandma's unknown rose. One year I discovered that one of my weakest floribundas had actually been growing in a corrugated steel pot for the last thirty years. But the most unsettling discovery for me was a Caribbean Santeria talisman I found buried deep under the hybrid tea 'Josephine Baker'.

If you are going to transplant a rose, all you need is a pair of pruners to cut back the plant; a spade—a shovel with a flat and sharp blade for cutting the roots; and a spading fork—a spade-like tool, but with four straight prongs for lifting the bush out of the ground.

First, pick a cloudy day without wind. Better yet, a nice cool misty morning is perfect. Have the new planting site ready before the rose is uprooted. There is going to be some element of shock to the bush, and the less time the plant has to sit out of the ground, the better. Prepare the new hole as you would if you were planting a new rose (see **April**).

Next, cut back the shrub to a manageable size you can handle in the move. If you want to preserve the height of the shrub or the lengths of the climbing canes you so carefully cultivated over the years, then eliminate all twiggy growth and bundle all of the strongest canes together using a strong, but soft twine like jute. By bundling the canes, you will have more control of the plant as you move it. But you can also cut the canes back to as short as 6 inches or a foot. Remember how short the new bare root plants are when they arrive from the nursery?

While the plant is still in the ground, use a spade to cut the roots. Encircle the plant about a foot or so from the center with sharp cuts, pushing down to a depth as far as the spade will penetrate. With the spading fork, gently lift the pruned rose from the earth. With your pruners, cut any roots remaining intact that might be holding the rose in place. A root ball with soil attached will be difficult to create, so don't bother. Shake off all of the soil and move the rose bare-rooted.

The older rose is, the more difficult it will be to find a recognizable root system. I've moved some that had just large knots of wood with only a few feeder roots, very small and fine, up near the surface. With these, I cut most of the woody root, making it much easier to replant the rose in a new hole.

Sometimes you get more than one plant out of an older bush. Over the years the bud unions seem to divide as the crown of the rose spreads out. In these instances, you can break one plant into many, as long as there is

A YEAR OF ROSES

sufficient root system to support each new piece. This is especially true for roses on their own roots.

I find it easy to lift the rose from one spot, carry it on the spading fork, and place it directly into the hole. This method disturbs the roots as little as possible.

If your planning to move a rose a great distance (greater than, say, from the back yard to the front yard),it would be best to keep the plant bare-root. Wrap the roots in wet newspapers or sphagnum. Allowing the roots to dry can be fatal to the rose. Alternatively, you could pot up the rose and leave it the way indefinitely. But you may have trouble finding a pot big enough. Besides, pots and soil are heavy and they take up space. Whichever way you decide to move the transplant, you should get it to its new home as quickly as possible.

Once you have planted the rose in a hole prepared with rich organic soil, water it. **Give the rose a bucket of some of your home-brewed manure tea at each watering**. (Read about planting in **April**, and tea in **May**). The last step in this procedure is to give the rose a thick layer of mulch, making sure that when the freezing weather finally arrives you mound up around the crown of the plant (see **December**).

In addition to transplanting, you can also plant *new* bare-root roses now. Autumn planting always seemed like a scary science project to me. But having once done it and discovering how much easier my spring gardening schedule became, I now prefer planting this time of year.

When I first started growing roses, there were only a handful of rose nurseries that would ship bare-root roses. As with other aspects of gardening, the tradition in this country has long been that spring is the *only* time to plant roses, autumn planting being reserved exclusively for spring flowering bulbs and winter annuals. Today, there are many nurseries shipping bare-root and potted roses throughout the country for fall planting. Bare-root or potted, autumn planting is recommended for the entire country. The weather is cool yet the soil is still warm, excellent for encouraging root growth.

Throughout our temperate and warm climate zones (the Southeast, Gulf Coast, Southwest, California, Pacific Northwest) this is not only the preferred time to plant, it's the *best* time to plant a rose. Planting can go on from now right through the winter and into spring. My gardener friends in coastal South Carolina complain that spring doesn't stick around long enough for spring planted roses to get a good start. The suddenness of summer-like temperatures in spring can sometimes deliver a fatal shock to a newly planted rose. Newly planted roses do best with the longest and coolest possible growing period. Wherever you garden, autumn planting will give your new roses an opportunity to grow strong roots, in preparation for next spring's top growth. **This is especially important to guarantee success with bare-root roses.**

In November, even though the bare-root rosebush you receive appears dormant, small fibrous roots will still develop after the rose is planted. In addition to this, the rose will begin to grow at the earliest possible time in the spring.

The first time I planted in autumn, I didn't enjoy it. I placed the orders in September and by late November the roses still hadn't arrived. For all I knew, snow and freezing weather could've been right around the corner. Needless to say, I lost sleep with every forecast of approaching cold fronts. It was the week after Thanksgiving, during a nasty storm, when the roses finally arrived. There wasn't any snow, but ice covered everything. Fortunately, while I was waiting, I dug the holes and prepared the sites where all of these roses were to go. I had learned a valuable lesson from this.

**This is how I recommend preparing for late arrivals:** Dig the holes while the soil is dry and frost free, the same as you would for spring planting (see **April**). In addition to adding compost to the hole and surrounding soil piles, add two large handfuls of perlite and mix it in well. Perlite is crushed-up pumice, available from your local garden center and sold as an additive to houseplant soil mixes. If your garden is in danger of becoming frozen, perlite keeps the soil in the new holes workable even though the rest of the garden is beginning to freeze. The crushed pumice will also improve the aeration quality of the soil. To further prevent the holes from freezing, mulch the entire planting area with leaves and straw. Throw it on nice and thick.

Many times since my first experience (I'm now a devout autumn planter), I've had to lift icy layers of leaves from the spot where the pre-dug holes were. Underneath this mulch is always workable soil, enabling me to plant the roses despite the frozen state of the rest of the garden.

When the roses finally arrive, plant them exactly the same way you would in the spring. The only difference would be the pruning of the top part of the plant. In warmer zones, where there isn't going to be a freeze, go ahead and prune as you would if you were planting in the spring. In colder regions, don't prune the tops at all, but only the roots.

Water and cover the roses entirely with a loose dry mulch, such as small wood chips. I have found that any part of the plant sticking out of the mulch will die back as a result of exposure to cold winter winds. If you are in an area that doesn't freeze but is exposed to windy conditions, mulch to protect the new roses from winter winds.

Once your garden freezes, there is no need to water until spring. If you're in an area where the ground doesn't freeze or there is an extended dry warm spell, keep an eye on your new arrivals. Water them weekly with manure tea.

Suppose the roses arrived and you can't plant them, or you couldn't pre-dig the garden. You'll need to get the roses into cold storage for the duration of the winter. The best option is to store them through the winter *in their boxes* in a cold cellar, in the garage, or on a cold porch. Keep the box of roses away from heaters, boilers, and the warming rays of the sun. Don't forget to check on them periodically to make sure that the roots don't dry out—they shouldn't if the box is kept cool and the plastic wrap around the roses is undisturbed. If you don't have space in your house or garage to store the roses, you could do what a couple of amateur gardeners on City Island, the Bronx (an island in Long Island Sound), had to do when they were taken by surprise. One very cold November morning, an early Christmas present arrived: a dozen bare-root rosebushes. They immediately created a raised bed garden.

Now this wasn't a carefully planned design, but a garden designed out of necessity. They had a large pile of leftover compost in a full sun location, just waiting to be put to use. These aspiring rosarians added to the compost whatever soil they could find at the local discount store. The bagged organic potting soils available this time of the year were mixed in and turned over with the compost, raising the bed to about 20 inches high. This was enough to plant the roses.

Raised beds can be an attractive addition to any garden, as well as a practical solution to many planting problems. With my friends, their new raised bed not only solved the problem of what to do with the late arrivals it also added a new element to their design. From a practical point of view, a raise bed can also be a way of making use of an area in your garden with poor drainage and especially poor soil.

For many in Houston, the easiest way to deal with their "gumbo" soil (the local term used to describe their thick, muck-like soil) is to grow roses in raised beds. Raised beds are a solution for growing beautiful roses in gardens in rocky areas as well as in flood-prone coastal regions.

The design—height, size, and shape of the bed—is completely up to your style and budget. The materials to create raised beds are numerous. Railroad ties, logs, stone, bricks, or even cinder blocks are all possibilities. Companion plants could be used to define the raised bed, soften the design, or add elements of color, fragrance, and texture to your design. Use them either on their own to define the bed or in combination with the material you use to create the bed. Lavender spilling over a wall would provide a fragrant edge to your roses. Lavender, a classic companion to roses, is often misused in gardens. On top of a wall, or along the slopes of a raised bed would give this perennial herb the excellent drainage it requires in order to do well. Other possible combinations could be nasturtiums cascading over railroad ties; marjoram, oregano, and thyme growing out of crevices or creating a fragrant and tasty edge to a raised bed. Dwarf boxwood would add a touch of class and classic formality to your raised bed design.

If you are building the garden over a natural soil surface, then a height of two feet would be ideal. The natural soil level should be sufficient for adequate drainage. You can also add rubble, gravel, or break up the surface to further improve the drainage before you add your planting mix.

You can also design a raised bed that is really just for decorative purposes, such as defining the boundary between the garden and a pathway. These beds can be as low as 6 inches (or whatever the thickness of the material you use to create the wall).

With raised beds built over a concrete or macadam surface, care should be taken to allow for drainage. Either break up the surface or add a layer of rubble to the hard surface.

The higher you raise the bed, the more exposed the sides will be to the elements. As with container gardens, more frequent watering may be needed. I would also recommend adding drainage holes at various heights along the walls of a higher bed.

A careful selection of roses can make the raised bed a very beautiful addition to your garden, as well as an interesting one. A raised bed built off a wall of your house, or behind a retaining wall for erosion control, can become a showcase for ground cover roses. With names like 'Flower Carpet' and 'Purple Pavement', these roses are shrub roses that tend to grow closer to the ground rather than mounding high like other roses. There are many varieties of these ever-blooming shrub roses available today, all capable of producing cascades of blooms on lax canes, perfect for creating an effect of roses spilling over the walls. There are many miniature roses that look great when allowed to grow freely from a raised bed. In fact, a raised bed is the best way to use miniature roses in the garden. Instead of having to stoop low to enjoy these beauties, now you can grow them at a comfortable level. Of course, any modern or old rose will grow and thrive in a raised bed garden, as well. There are no limits to your choices.

Sometimes you can even plant roses right into a retaining wall or the wall of the raised bed. This was beautifully done at the Morris Arboretum in Philadelphia. Several bushes of the miniature rose 'Cinderella' were planted into soil pockets of a stone wall—an ideal way to display the tiny white blooms of this micro-mini.

Other design concepts, such as pillars, arches, and festoons can all be incorporated into a raised rose garden.

A raised bed is one way of dealing with a poor soil situation, especially if you have layers of rocks or, like in Houston, a sticky soil. Sometimes you can avoid the added expense of a raised bed by deep tilling—loosening up the existing soil, adding organics, bringing air back to the root zone, and ultimately improving its drainage.

This is a very physical job—backbreaking, to be honest with you—but it works. Turn over the soil with a spading fork folding in the mulch from this season. Not only are you aerating the soil, you're also exposing buried weed seeds and insect larvae to the cold air, as well as turning fungal spores deep into the soil, away from the surface.

You can start this job as early as September if you're in a snow-belt region and do it anytime the soil is not frozen or wet. I wouldn't feel comfortable recommending this if your garden is going to freeze in the immediate future. If that's the case, then it's too late to work the soil. Instead, do this after you have finished your spring pruning and just before adding your new layer of mulch.

If you have a month or so before freezing, or if your average winter temperature is in the forties of fifties, then do this now. Wait until you've finished all activity (cutting back of the shrubs, deadheading, etc.) in the beds so that you won't have to walk on the  freshly turned soil. Your goal is to open and aerate the soil, walking on it after you're done would only defeat this purpose and cause compaction.

Add well-aged manure or bone meal to the beds as you work the soil. This is also the perfect time to add lime if your soil has been too acidic (low number on the pH scale), or to add sulfur if the soil has too much alkalinity (high number on the pH scale). These additives are slow acting and would have the entire winter to be absorbed by your garden.

Turning over the soil also sends organic material from the surface deeper to the root zones of your roses. An alternative to this vigorous workout would be to gently fold leaf mold under the roses. Pile a spade full, or two, of leaf mold (well composted, chopped up leaves) on the soil surface and gently work it into the soil. Try getting as close to the main stems as possible.

An annual session with the spading fork promotes strong growth and strong backs. If you can't be bothered, or if you have under-planted your roses with companion plants, it would still be a good idea to at least spear the open ground with a spading fork, aerating the soil around all the roots. Even this little bit of effort will help improve the growing capacity of your soil.

Sometimes however, more drastic changes are needed in the garden if you notice that your roses are consistently not doing well.

For many years I would watch the garden come into full bloom and lush growth only to watch it quickly wither away as soon as temperatures remained consistently hot. After many frustrating seasons dealing with this phenomenon, I pulled up two rosebushes, both from the same bed. One plant was quite old, with hardly any root system apart from a large wooden taproot and lots of fibrous roots near the surface of the soil. The other plant was only in the garden for two growing seasons. Likewise there was hardly any root development from the original roots, but there were a considerable number of small roots growing very near the surface.

What this told me was that the soil was not conducive to root growth except near the surface, where there was considerable mulch, lots of particles and organic material. This would explain why problems increased as soon as the temperatures rose. The roots doing all the work were too close to the surface of the soil, exposed to the heat and drought and damaged from cultivation of the soil and compaction brought on by visitors walking through the beds. This damage resulted in the dropping of foliage and poor flower production as the season progressed and the days became hotter.

The solution was to excavate and replace the soil with a new, friable mix. **The new soil mix is composed of the following:**
- 60 percent sandy top soil
- 30 percent compost
- 10 percent sand

In the beds where this backbreaking project has been completed I have not lost a rosebush, even through the hardest winters. In fact, one autumn when I needed to transplant from the new beds, I was thrilled to encounter a huge mass of fibrous feeder roots when I removed a rose that had been in the ground only for one season.

November brings cooler weather to everyone, especially in the south. Along with this change of temperature is the appearance of another form of a thrip, known as the red-banded thrip. More of a sub-tropical pest, this tiny pest is found often in tropical fruit trees, especially mango and avocado. It's during the dry weather of the autumn that the red-banded thrip feeds on rose foliage. You may think you have spider mites, since the symptoms are very similar—the tops of the leaves look dusty and gray. The insect is actually on the underside of the leaf, they're very tiny and black—sometimes displaying a red stripe, sort of like a belt, on their tiny

$^1/_8$-inch body. They will cause the leaves to drop and they also leave behind a disgusting black sooty mold.

Red-banded thrips can be controlled with beneficial insects as well as pyrethrums. However, if you're patient enough, as the weather cools, these critters will retreat.

November is one of the wettest months for the northeast and a time with extreme weather patterns throughout the country. There's always the threat of snow, late hurricanes and nor'easters (basically a cold weather hurricane, common to the east coast) bringing lots of wind, rain, and floods, and roller-coaster temperature readings. In 1995, the first truly cold morning in my garden arrived on November 9. That same year there was an inch of snow in Dallas on November 28, while in New York City the temperatures were hovering in the mid-60s. On November 29, 4 inches of snow fell in New York City, with the remainder of the week fluctuating only into the high 30s. And though winter had arrived nearly a month early for us, the west coast of North America was experiencing record-breaking rain and windstorms, spring-like weather was happening in Denver, Des Moines was under a deep freeze, and they were posting freeze warnings for areas just north of New Orleans and in northern Florida.

Since we never know what November has in store for us, it's advisable to take advantage of every nice gardening day during this month. Make preparations for winter, for once the snow falls or the ground freezes, there is little to do in the garden but enjoy the beauty of the snow-covered landscape.

The day after that first snowfall in early November, it was magical to wander through the garden, with foliage and flowers still visible beneath the snow. The natural architecture was accented with the weight of the snow, and the display of arching canes from the tall shrubs and climbers was duplicated by the man-made features such as arches, festoons, and the series of highlighted lattice patterns

The hips of *Rosa canina* and 'Carefree Beauty' were vivid red and orange, and cardinals and juncos were easy to spot as they fed on these hips and others throughout the rose garden. A squirrel hung onto a cane of 'Coral Creeper' with the grace of a circus acrobat, grabbing ripe rose hips and then quickly burying them under the snow.

There are many roses, from all classes, that are good hip producers. If you stopped deadheading at the end of the summer then you should now be rewarded with a hip display from many of the modern ever-blooming roses. 'Autumn Sunset', a modern shrub that could also be used as a climb-ing rose, produces large orange hips that will stay on the plant the entire

*Cover this arbor with climbing roses for a fragrant entrance into the garden.*

winter. My specimen of this rose is trained to grow up through my Blue Atlas Cedar. The display of pumpkin-colored hips in combination with the gray-blue needles of the conifer is quite nice.

The best hip displays happen on species roses and their hybrids. The colors of rose hips range from green to blackish-purple to vermillion to bright cherry red. The sizes and shapes of rose hips are various too—from egg shaped to elegant fluted forms. Some are smooth and shiny while others are dull and bristly. One of the most interesting hips is the bristly and foreboding hip of *Rosa roxburghii*.

This hip is covered with small bristles, earning the rose the nicknames of "Burr Rose" and "Chestnut Rose." It does resemble the casing of a chestnut, but only smaller. The hips of *Rosa roxburghii* begin to develop in early summer (this rose blooms before the peak of hybrid teas) and stay on the bush until mid-summer. When these hips fall they're still green with the remains of the sepals firmly attached. The mature hip is egg-shaped, measuring 1 inch wide by ¹/₂ inch high.

*Rosa × micrugosa*, a hybrid between *Rosa rugosa* and *Rosa roxburghii* is a tall spring blooming shrub with large pale pink single flowers. Its hips have the exact look of the 'Chestnut Rose' with the red color of *Rosa rugosa*.

Some other species of notable hip displays: *Rosa arkansana*, red, pear-shaped, shiny; *Rosa virginiana*, red, shiny, half-inch wide, free of sepals; *Rosa villosa*, also known as the "apple bearing rose," dark red, bristly, pear shaped, very tasty; *Rosa canina*, egg shaped, bright red; *Rosa bracteata*, round, orange-red, bristly; *Rosa spinosissima* 'Altaica', black, round, shiny; *Rosa sericea* 'Redwing', scarlet, shiny, small and globular; *Rosa setigera*, small, orange-red, round.

As if knowing that the end of the season had arrived, the cold hardy old garden roses were losing their foliage and the modern roses proudly

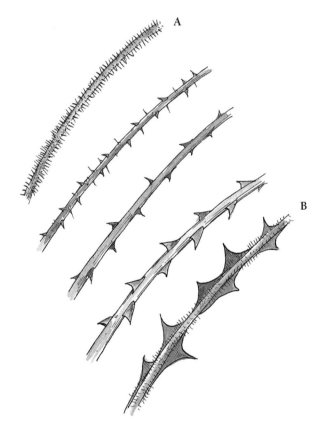

*In the autumn the natural architecture of the garden is more obvious. Prickles can range from bristle-like (A) to broad-winged forms (B).*

displayed their frozen blooms on leafless branches. Actually these cold-hardy plants were preparing for the long onslaught of winter—hardening themselves off, rapidly becoming dormant.

The warm weather roses, on the other hand (my teas, Chinas, Bourbons, and Noisettes), had been on suicide missions all month, toying with fate. Yesterday, red, succulent new growth was beautifully displayed high above the lush foliage, and many plants were full of large nodding blooms. Huge sprays of tea rose blooms were overflowing the pots. 'Mermaid' was aglow with lemon yellow blossoms and sending long canes even higher up the lattice pavilion (as the days became shorter, the new canes seemed to be getting longer and longer). These roses didn't have a clue as to what was around the corner. This was their final gasp of glory—their last hurrah. 'Duchesse de Brabant', 'Monsieur Tillier', and "Smith's Parish" were caught in the act of blooming. Today they're pale and freeze-dried. Visible through the snow. But they're still beautiful.

---

## RECOMMENDED MEMBERSHIP

The Canadian Rose Society
  334 Queen Mary Road—Apt. 504
  Kingston, Ontario K7M 7E7
  **www.canadianrosesociety.org**
  Various membership levels

Central Florida Heritage Rose Society
  **http://hometown.aol.com/cartisano/cfhrs.html**

Dallas Area Historical Rose Group
  PO Box 831448
  Richardson, TX 75083-1148
  Various membership levels
  **www.antiqueroses.org**

Manhattan Rose Society
  Rosemarie Murphy
  1978B Alwood Drive
  Bethlehem, PA 18018
  various membership levels
  **www.manhattanrosesociety.org**

Nashville Rose Society (various membership levels)
  **www.nashvillerosesociety.com**

Help Me Find Roses
  **www.helpmefind.com/roses** (database of 26,000 roses)

# DECEMBER

You can begin long-lasting relationships shoveling manure, especially when it's for the love of roses. The horse stables in Leonia, New Jersey, are my preferred manure source. They've got some of the best horse stuff around. But then, I imagine that everyone has their favorite pile.

If the snow hasn't buried the rose beds completely by December, I spread manure (cow or horse) around the roses, taking care not to let it touch the canes. It's not really intended as a winter blanket, but as a slow release soil conditioner for next year. Through the winter the manure slowly breaks down, releasing beneficial bacteria into the soil which will in turn eventually supply the new root growth in early spring with much needed nutrients. Before we see any activity among the leaf buds on the rose canes, the roots are beginning to absorb nutrients from the soil to support the growth that will occur as a result of warmer spring weather and pruning. So, start spreading manure, use it as fresh as you can stand!

If I can't make it to the manure pile, I at least spread compost over all the areas of exposed soil, especially where I have just planted my bulbs. It's such a waste to see all those piles of leaves left on the curb for pick-up. I recently invested in a small shredder/chipper and I've been known to raid the neighbor's leaf pile in search of leaves to shred and spread through my garden. Everyone around me is so obsessed with cleaning the garden of all fallen leaves. I spend this time in early December shredding and spreading leaves, bulking up the organic content of the garden soil. And it looks so nice!

This month the rainy season begins along the west coast, the snow piles high in the upper Midwest, ice storms sneak in and out of Texas, and the overnight freezes keep Floridians in touch with reality. For me, this is the month that arguments can start in the rose garden.

I learned that when you tell someone to cut back roses to hip height, it's important to specify whose hips you're referring to, especially when one volunteer is 6 feet tall and the other one is just under 5 feet tall. But that was several years ago. I no longer recommend cutting roses back for winter; my garden is a more peaceful place ever since—and now I may even find a rose or two to cut for Christmas.

Cutting back rose bushes in December only accomplishes one thing: they look better over the winter when they are cut to an even height. But it's not necessarily a better treatment for the plants.

Cutting the rosebushes before a freeze will only encourage dormant buds to awaken, producing new growth—growth that will only die back with the next freeze. So, it's best for the plant if you leave them alone until it's time for spring pruning. However, if you have to look at your collection of irregular looking sticks all winter, then I would cut back to an even height. But remember, you will still have to return in the spring to do a thorough pruning.

The only gardeners who should be cutting back roses during the winter, to improve the quality of the plant, are those gardeners living in warm areas where roses don't go into full dormancy. If this is you, wait until the end of this month or even January, before starting to prune your roses, and follow the pruning recommendations given in **February**.

When I first became a rosarian, my mother told me that I was going to spend a great deal of time worrying. She was right, all through the growing season and especially as winter approaches. I keep a watchful eye on the weather as winter officially begins: worrying about the effects of inevitable ice storms on the garden, watching for the possibility of a freeze and thaw and, most of all, praying for snow. Snow is good for the garden, especially roses. It's Mother Nature's mulch. A blanket of snow in the garden is the best insulation you can ask for when the winter wind is blowing cold and icy.

An ice storm is the opposite. **The potential for lethal damage to the rose garden from an ice storm is astounding.** As beautiful as they might appear, the weight of ice-covered canes can tear even the strongest climbing roses down to the size of small shrubs. The exposed, dormant buds of any rose that might have started to grow during a warm spell will die in an ice storm. Coastal communities, such as Brooklyn and most of the Eastern Seaboard, around the Great Lakes, and in regions where it's never quite cold enough to sustain snow, ice can be a common occurrence. Perhaps more threatening to the garden than ice is the fluctuation in temperatures during the winter—from very cold to mild, a common occurrence in my neck of the woods.

In preparation for this, my December mornings in the rose garden begin with trips to the wood chip pile—one source of an excellent winter mulch. Once the temperature starts hovering in the freezing range and the ground has frozen, I protect my tender and weaker rosebushes with piles of dry wood chips. My goal is to protect them from the seesaw weather patterns of winter, which can tease an unsuspecting dormant bud into waking up. And to protect them from the winter sun and wind—both can cause the canes to dry out, a leading cause of winterkill.

I don't mound all the roses. That's way too much work. And, besides, if they all should need protection, then perhaps they're the wrong roses for my garden. I have six thousand plants - that's too many to mulch (my volunteers have gone into hibernation). However, this is not to say you shouldn't mulch all of your roses. I'm in zone 7, and winters here are cold but not as severe as further north. If you're in colder zones, then I would recommend mulching all budded roses, and maybe your smaller own root varieties. You should decide who you think needs, or deserves, an extra layer of protection. If you can manage to mulch all of your roses, then go for it! But remember, the further north you garden, or the more exposed you are to adverse winter weather, the more you should consider winter mulch.

The truth is, like most rosarians, I have some favorites that I couldn't bear to part with, even if they do need some extra winter TLC. I mulch the weakest-looking plants, as well as any unusual specimens from across the country, Europe, and Asia (until I'm sure of their hardiness), my tea and China roses, the musk rose, my collection of Bermuda Mystery Roses, and all roses newly planted in the autumn. Most hybrid teas, floribundas, climbers, shrub roses, rugosas, most species, and the European old garden roses (gallicas, albas, damasks, Portlands) are able to survive the winter weather in my zone, so I don't bother with mulching these roses. A winter mulch will protect the roses that are not accustomed to going into a winter dormancy, such as the teas, Chinas, and many of the Noisettes. Without a cover they could die completely. The mulch will at least save their roots, bud unions (if they have one), and some of the wood above ground. I can't possibly cover an entire plant if it's taller than 12 inches, so I make sure that at least the base area is protected.

Mounding (putting down winter mulch) is done to protect the plant from the ravages of winter. But mounding with the wrong materials can also lead to a higher incidence of dieback, usually brought on by disease. One of these is canker, the same fungal disease you'll encounter during the spring pruning (see **March**).

The fungus that causes canker thrives in moist and cool conditions— exactly the environment you create when you mound wet soil and manure up against a rose cane. Be sure you remove all diseased-looking and dead canes before mounding with a mulch. And, most important, use a dry mulch.

*In cold climates a dry material like wood chips or shredded
leaves can be used to create a mound around the base of roses
requiring winter protection.*

Examples of dry mulches are wood chips, straw, pine needles, salt hay,
and evergreen branches. **I prefer wood chips, the smallest size, or ground
up leaves mixed with garden soil.**

I pile mulch nearly a foot, sometimes a foot and a half (for those extra
special varieties) right onto the bush; the chips spill to about the same distance wide. To make sure that all of the nooks and crannies of the plant
are filled, I very carefully shake the chips into the center of the plant
around each cane.

Which plants need mounding can vary from climate to climate. Some
climates can be merciless on any rose, no matter how cold-hardy it is
supposed to be. If you are in a tough winter situation, keep in mind that
budded roses will not do as well as own-root roses in conditions of severe
winter weather. Once an own-root rose is strongly established it will need
less winter protection than a budded rose will. But it still wouldn't hurt to
think SNOW! **Once your roses are under the snow, they are as safe as
they could possibly be.**

My brothers try to grow roses in Boulder, Colorado. The winters of
Boulder are actually more mild than those of New Jersey, except that there
are many "false starts" to spring. It's not uncommon to have sixty degree
weather one day followed by icy cold winds the next. It's easy to protect
the shrub type roses here with mounding, but what about climbers and

larger shrub roses? The same can be said for a garden along the shores of Lake Michigan or any of the Great Lakes, or any garden near the sea. The icy winds that blow in these locations will cause severe, often fatal, damage to large growing roses, often limiting a gardener's choices to very few, if any at all, of these varieties.

One solution to this problem is to build windbreaks. One way would be to make this a permanent part of your design, such as a solid fence, a high wall, or tall evergreen hedges. Or, you cold construct a winter barrier of burlap fencing. Using tall oak stakes and four foot high pieces of burlap, build a fence around your taller roses. A rosarian in New Hampshire has had great success with protecting his less hardy roses by using the very thin Styrofoam sheets, originally used to wrap refrigerators and other appliances for shipping, as a barrier.

In Minnesota, the dedicated rosarians of this northern state have perfected a way to get their large shrubs and climbers through the winter. Drive through Minneapolis and you'll see the rosarians doing the "Minnesota Tip." Yes, it is sort of a dance that all Minnesota rosarians swear by, and they all do it in their rose gardens in early October.

## THE MINNESOTA TIP

Large shrub-type roses (English Roses, for example) and Climbing roses:

- A few days before you "tip," water the plants well, to loosen the soil
- Spray the rose with a dormant oil spray or lime-sulfur
- Only prune enough to make the rose a manageable size
- Bundle the rose together
- Dig a trench the size of the bundled rose right alongside the rose; dig towards the base of the rose, making your trench deep enough to bury the rose under two to 3 inches of soil and wide enough to fit the bundle
- Loosen the root system with a spading fork (below the bud union if it's a budded rose)
- Bend the bundled rose (from the root system, not at the stem) into the trench
- You may want to peg the rose to secure it in the trench (your spading fork can serve as a temporary peg)
- Bury the plant with two to 3 inches of garden soil
- Leave your rose like this until the ground has frozen
- After the soil is frozen, bury the entire trench with up to 2 feet of mulch. Cover with evergreen branches and/or chicken wire to keep the leaves from blowing away
- Wait until mid-April before you start uncovering

Sounds serious, huh? You don't have to live in Minnesota to do this, but I think the rosarians from Minneapolis would appreciate some recognition and credit, and please, don't ever refer to it as the "Minnesota Dip!"

These rosarians are truly in love with their modern shrub roses, but it's way too much work for me. After one winter, I'd look for alternative roses to grow. Maybe more cold hardy old garden roses such as gallica roses. Unfortunately, these are only once-blooming roses. For ever-bloomers, I would investigate the Canadian Explorer roses, Morden shrub roses (also bred in Canada for winter hardiness), or perhaps some of the Buck roses. These are ever-blooming roses bred by the late Griffith Buck of Ames, Iowa. Dr. Buck focused on creating roses that would produce fragrant, large roses on shrubs capable of surviving the winters of Ames without any strenuous winter protection. I've grown many of his roses, several are quite beautiful. Among my favorites are: 'Distant Drums', 'Hi Neighbor', 'Carefree Beauty' (it really is!) and 'Prairie Princess'. Whichever roses you end up selecting for a cold northern climate, remember, you'll have better success with the ones that are on their own roots.

Up in Saratoga, New York, there's a wonderful public rose garden on the property of the artists' retreat, Yadoo. This garden, the Katrina Trask Rose Garden, features a beautiful pergola of white Ionic columns that's covered with climbing roses.

The Yadoo garden volunteers have been very successful with climbers 'New Dawn', 'Blaze', and 'Crimson Rambler' (this particular variety was the original rose used to cove the entire pergola in 1901)in this zone 5 garden. They don't go through as much work as our friends in the Midwest, instead, they bring the canes down to the ground, bundle them together, and then bury the canes under a pile of straw and leaves. 'Crimson Rambler' is especially susceptible to powdery mildew, so it is highly recommended that the canes of the roses are sprayed with lime-sulfur or dormant oil. And, it wouldn't be a bad idea to throw in some rodent bait, or maybe spray the canes and the mulch with an animal repellent. It would be extremely frustrating to discover that after all this work to save the rose from the winter it only dies because some little critter decided to gnaw at the bark in search of water.

Every winter I'm concerned that the canes of ramblers I've trained into festoons over the hybrid tea beds will die back, since they're exposed to the elements. For protection from cold winds and ice of winter, I tie evergreen boughs up the pillars and around the chains. This is a great use of discarded holiday trees and wreaths. The greens make excellent protective wraps for climbing roses. The immediate result—huge hanging boas of green in the rose garden—add an interesting feature to the winter garden.

*You may want to protect your festoons from cold winter winds.*
*Wrap salt hay or evergreen boughs around the canes. Cover the*
*whole chain with burlap to keep the materials in place.*

For several seasons I worked in a very elaborate rose garden designed on a narrow peninsula in East Hampton, New York. The garden spanned from just behind the tall ocean sand dunes to the shore of a wide tidal pond. The roses were exposed to cold winds from the ocean as well as winds from the pond, so it was absolutely necessary that they were wrapped every winter. To insure their survival, first the canes were tied in tight to the structure. Next, evergreen boughs were wrapped around the roses and whatever structure they were trained to (arches, columns, posts). The greens were further secured with a burlap wrap.

In other similar situations, the thin Styrofoam wrapping was used in place of the burlap.

Another garden that I work in has a tennis court fence completely covered with roses and only a half-mile from the ocean. To protect this collection, I push evergreen boughs into the fence, completely covering all canes as well as the fence giving the tennis fence a wonderful plush green look for the winter.

Some people decorate their gardens for the holidays with plastic Santas. I wrap my tree roses with salt hay. It's not really a holiday decoration. It just works out that I wrap my tree roses in time for the Christmas holidays. They give the garden a festive look, but my straw-ladies, as I refer to them, remain in the rose garden long after Christmas as permanent winter ornaments.

I've tested tree roses in the past by not wrapping them, to see if they will indeed survive the winter. Older standards with their gnarled, woody bud unions survive the winter better than younger ones. And, if the tree rose is grafted onto a *Rosa rugosa* stem rather than 'Dr. Huey' or any other typically used, it will be more tolerant of winter conditions and more likely to survive the freezing temperatures and winds. However, tree roses are expensive, and I wouldn't recommend taking the chance with their survival over the winter if you're in a cold zone. If your trees are in moveable containers, the best thing to do would be to move them into a garage, cellar, shed, window wells, or any other place that will allow them to stay cold but not exposed to the winds, ice, and unstable temperatures. And don't forget to water them! If you grow them in a more permanent situation in the garden and you have severe winter weather, then it will be necessary to protect them.

They grow tree roses in the Katrina Trask Rose Garden. To get them through the winter, the volunteers bury all of the standards in the compost pile for the entire winter. This means that each autumn, the plants are actually dug up and removed from the rose garden. In other cold weather gardens I've seen similar techniques to the "Minnesota Tip", leaving the trees in the garden but storing them on their sides, roots loosened and the tree pulled down into a trench or simply resting on the ground under a pile of mulch. Both of these techniques require more space than you might have in your garden, and this can be a very messy job. In my opinion, these roses aren't worth the trouble.

Wrapping the trees with salt hay (a harvested marsh grass, available in bales at local garden centers) has worked for me, getting my tree roses through the coldest winters. If you need to prune the tops, go ahead, but just prune enough to make the top area fit in your design for protection. You'll need to prune again in the spring for shaping. The first thing to do is to add two more stakes, at least as tall, if not taller, than the tree rose to help support the extra weight of the winter protection. There is always a danger that the tree roses can break from the added weight of the salt hay and snow. I use 6-foot-long tomato stakes. Next, shove hay into the center of the top area, making a nice bird's nest-type protection around the bud unions (tree roses usually have three of them at top). This is the most important are to protect. Then, wrap the entire tree stem with sheets of hay (it usually peels out the bundle in sheets) from the top down. This

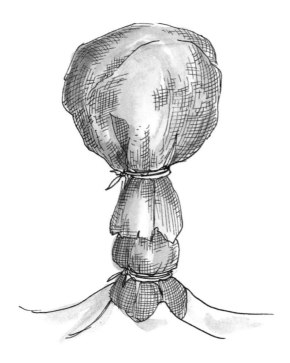

*A tree rose wrapped for the winter.*

gives the top part a little more support and protects this long cane from possible wind damage.

Wrap the long tree stem from top to base, tying the hay into place and eventually spreading out around the root zone. Stuff as much hay as possible in around all of the branches of the rose, giving the effect of a wild hairdo for your "straw-ladies". Make sure all of the hay is securely tied so that it doesn't blow away of fall off in a storm. You might want to consider the finishing touch of a winter bonnet made of burlap and tied around the top of the tree trees to keep the straw in place.

**More often than not, the biggest winter problem with containerized roses in a cold climate is wondering whether or not the container will survive the winter.** A potted rose often dies over the winter because the terra-cotta pot it was growing in shattered from freezing and thawing, thus exposing the root system to the freezing cold.

A fellow Brooklynite has a garden of potted miniature roses, all on her outdoor porch. To insure their survival through the winter, she stores them under the porch during the winter. In this crawl space, the temperature hovers in the low 30s during the coldest periods. This gives the roses their needed cold period and yet it is a stable temperature for the roots and pots.

Another way of saving potted roses through the winter might be to cluster them in a shaded corner of your terrace or patio, touching rim to rim. Stuff an insulating material, such as newspaper, Styrofoam, salt hay, straw, leaves, or evergreen boughs in among the spaces between the pots. To finish off the winter protection, create a wall of the same insulation around the exposed side of the corralled pots.

**Check you containers regularly, depending on how warm it gets, to make sure that the soil hasn't dried out.** Apart from freezing roots, the chief reason why so many potted roses fail to survive the winter is drought.

It's risky to assume that my potted tea roses (remember, I'm talking about real tea roses, not hybrid teas) will survive the winter without assistance, given the expected dips into subfreezing temperatures within the next month.

At the beginning of December, or as soon as these roses have been shut down by cold weather, I remove them from the pots and plant them in the garden. Like the other teas and Chinas planted in the ground, I bury the ex-potted tea roses with a winter mulch. They could also be left potted and brought into a cool storage area, where they should be allowed to go dormant but not dry.

With all of this winter protection, it's important to remember to first spray your roses with a dormant oil or lime-sulfur whether you're going to cover them, bury them, or store them in a safe spot. This is going to be your first step to preventing the spread of pests in the garden for next season.

The real test of your talent as a rosarian will be to bring a plant from the frozen garden into full bloom by Valentine's Day, and to do it indoors.

The winter months are best for indoor rose growing. You don't have to have extensive greenhouses and sophisticated equipment to accomplish this. It's easy, and here's how to do it.

After the first cold snap, select a plant that will fit in your window. Be realistic now, and don't try digging up your prized hybrid tea or climber! A miniature rose would do perfect. Small China roses could be attractive indoors, too. Dig up your selection, or perhaps you'll have to chop it out of the frozen earth. Prune the roots enough to make it fit into a pot. (The size of the pot will depend on how much space you have indoors). Next, prune the top part and get rid of all remaining foliage. Be severe. I prune so that my indoor plant starts growing from just three canes.

One last step before bringing the plant into your house is to dip the plant in a soapy water solution (create "gray water" by swishing a bar of Ivory soap, or any other non-perfumed soap, in a bucket of water) and spray the canes with a dormant oil solution. This will lessen the chances that you might bring in unwanted guests. It's a good idea to clean your windowsill with a bleach solution to rid it of any possible plant pests. Corners are especially favorite hiding spots for spider mites.

I prefer the look of clay, but that's a personal preference. Any pot will do, as long as you plant the rose up in a pot that gives the roots room to grow. A soil-less potting mix (available at any garden center) is fine. Or you can make your own mix using one part sand or perlite and one part potting soil.

A windowsill is the minimum space requirement. However, you will need supplemental light. In the winter the sun is lower in the sky and the natural light is not intense enough for producing a bloom of the quality of the summer rose garden. This is why you must add the extra lighting.

Plant lights, or grow lights, will work, but regular fluorescent light bulbs are much less expensive and just as effective. Buy a two-foot, or four-foot fixture depending on how wide your window is. Get a fixture with a reflector that holds two bulbs. A fixture like this usually comes without bulbs, so you need to buy one warm bulb and one cool bulb (read the packaging of the bulbs, it will designate whether the bulb is warm or cool). This combination of bulbs is enough to create a beautiful window garden.

I set up my fixtures in the kitchen window, which is just wide enough to fit a two-foot fixture. I have three shelves in the window, and each shelf has its own light fixture. Under one two-foot lamp I can comfortably fit four 6-inch pots.

The kitchen window is very sunny all day long, and is also cool. Heat can spell disaster to a rose growing indoors, and even during the winter sunny window can become very warm. A temperature in the mid-to-low 50s at night and up to near 75 degrees Fahrenheit during the day is ideal.

The light fixtures should be able to be adjusted up and down. The lights should always be about 6 to 8 inches from the top of the roses. As the plants grow, you'll need to move your lights, to give the plants more room. You can do this easily by suspending the fixture on chains. **The duration of light is important as well.** I have the lights on timer set for fourteen hours daily to get the best rose blooms from my miniatures.

As with any outdoor garden, indoor roses will need good air circulation. Don't crowd the pots into corners, and leave some space between pots.

Potted roses dry out even faster indoors, so you'll need to check them daily. Water them when the soil is dry to the touch, making sure that the water goes all the way through to the bottom of the pot. To prevent the water from rushing down the sides of the pots, away from the center of the plant, I occasionally push chopsticks into the soil around the plant. This creates openings that allow water to get through to the entire root system. A daily misting with cool water is recommended to keep a higher level of humidity (inside heat tends to be dry, especially in apartments) and to ward off any curious spider mites. Keeping the pots on a gravel-filled tray, with water just below the top of the gravel, will help to raise the humidity.

For pest control, besides the regular mistings, break up a garlic clove and plant the smaller cloves into the soil, around the small rose bush. Simply push the flat end of the clove into the soil, leaving the tip exposed. Soon, green leaves will sprout, not only acting as a natural pesticide, warding off aphids and mites, but also serving as a tasty additive to soups, sauces, and salads. I harvest regularly by simply snipping tips as I need them.

A basic houseplant fertilizer (odorless, please!) will complete your setup. I begin fertilizing the roses roughly two weeks after I bring them in. This is about the time I begin to see growth. Continue feeding every two weeks with a solution that is half the recommended rate on the fertilizer jar. As an added treat, when I clean my orange juice containers or milk containers for recycling, I pour the rinse water onto my potted roses.

If you don't want to fuss with digging up your outdoor roses, there are many nurseries that will ship miniature roses in December in bud and bloom—they arrive with foliage and a few flowers. This is an easy way to start, but you'll need to repot them and give them lots of TLC to adjust to their new environment.

One of my favorite miniature roses is 'Sweet Chariot'. I love the fragrance of this mauve-colored, pompon shaped rose. It's easy to grow indoors, and each year it gets nicer and nicer. I bring in 'Sweet Chariot' from the garden Christmas week and by Valentine's Day I have an 8-inch pot overflowing with fragrant blooms. The clusters of blooms are on the ends of canes measuring over a foot and a half in length.

Don't try to keep the minis, or any other rose from your windowsill, indoors all year long. This takes a great deal of work to make it worthwhile, and that's not fun. The best place for the rose is outdoors. By late winter, I find that the sun is already becoming too warm indoors. That's when I cut back the plants and they go back into the garden as soon as I can dig a hole in the spring.

Bringing roses indoors for the winter is a way for us northern gardeners to extend the rose season to fill nearly the entire year. I look forward to December for that reason. But I still enjoy the chance to sit and enjoy the beauty of the winter garden.

As I sit among the dormant roses in the garden, I'm anxiously observing the cat and mouse game going on between the large, immature Red-tailed hawk (a winter resident) and the rabbits. The hawk, who has become very tame, is sitting close by on a low tree limb, and eyeing the rabbits as they prepare to feast on a juicy-looking cane of 'Frau Karl Druschki'. I think about how easy it would be to rustle the rabbits out into the open, feeling less guilty about being an accessory to the crime as they begin to nibble away on my prize rose.

Saving me from the horrible deed, a visitor to the garden passes by, disturbing the rabbits and sending the hawk in hot pursuit. I see a flash of white cottontails, and a flutter of enormous wings as I lose sight of the chase behind a clump of the 'Prairie Rose' on the hillside. I hear a dull thud. The hawk, obviously inexperienced, has landed headfirst into a pile of weeds, sans rabbit. Slightly stunned, but I suspect more embarrassed, he sets himself back up on the branch overhead. Oh, well, it looks as though it will be an interesting winter after all. Before heading inside, I dig up the miniature rose 'Sweet Chariot', now completely dormant. I prune it back and carefully shave the root ball to make it fit into an 8-inch clay pot. Back in my kitchen I set the rose under the light fixture in the window and start the season again.

Long after the sun has set I hear the click of the automatic timer and lights switch off, signaling the end of the day for my indoor rose garden. I take this cue to curl myself up on the sofa. And as I begin to read the newly arrived rose catalogs, I slowly start dreaming of my rose garden in the year to come.

---

## FOR MORE INFORMATION ON WINTER PROTECTION
Minnesota Rose Society
  www.minnesotarosesociety.org

## RECOMMENDED MEMBERSHIP
Heritage Roses Group
  $12/year
  This group is divided into 4 sub-groups
  Check the website for the group nearest you
  www.heritagerosesgroup.org

# GROWTH HABITS AND PRUNING DETAILS OF MAIN ROSE GROUPS

## ONCE-BLOOMING ROSES: SPECIES AND SPECIES HYBRIDS
*Habit:* There's a wide range of growth habits among species roses.
- Tall arching shrubs
- Long-caned climbers
- Compact upright shapes
- There are a few that have a tendency to grow out of bounds through root suckering and self-seeding.

After bloom, remove a few older canes to make room for new growth; do not remove too much or you may lose your hip display. In winter, after the hips have rotted or have been eaten by birds, thin out $1/3$ of the oldest wood to give the shrub a clean look. Prune when they become invasive.

## GALLICA
- sprawling shrubs
- freely suckering growth habits
- Some could make interesting ground cover plants.
- majority are medium height shrubs, though there are some capable of being trained as climbers and a few that are of a dwarf habit

After bloom, remove old wood to make room for new growth. Do not prune too much of hip producers during the season to preserve the hip display for autumn and winter. During winter, shorten all canes to various lengths to eliminate crossing and rubbing; trim back all side shoots to three or four bud eyes.

## DAMASK
- sprawling shrubs
- Some with tall, long arching branches that tend to fall over from the weight of the large roses.
- several varieties could be coaxed to climb with a little bit of persuasion

After bloom, remove old wood to make room for new growth. Do not prune too much of hip producers during the season to preserve the hip display for autumn and winter. During winter, shorten all canes to various lengths to eliminate crossing and rubbing; trim back all side shoots to three or four bud eyes.

## ALBA
- Mix of tall and medium sized, sprawling shrubs
- Some varieties have lax canes, can be trained onto pillars

After bloom, remove old wood to make room for new growth. Do not prune too much of hip producers during the season to preserve the hip display for autumn and winter. During winter, shorten all canes to various lengths to eliminate crossing and rubbing; trim back all side shoots to three or four bud eyes.

## CENTIFOLIA
- The plants are upright medium sized shrubs
- Weight of the fragrant roses cause many varieties to sprawl.

After bloom, remove old wood to make room for new growth. Do not prune too much of hip producers during the season to preserve the hip display for autumn and winter. During winter, shorten all canes to various lengths to eliminate crossing and rubbing; trim back all side shoots to three or four bud eyes.

## MOSS
- Some varieties are quite tall, others sprawl from the weight of the roses

After bloom, remove old wood to make room for new growth. Some old blooms may need to be shaken off or trimmed. Do not prune too much of hip producers during the season to preserve the hip display for autumn and winter. During winter, shorten all canes to various lengths to eliminate crossing and rubbing; trim back all side shoots to three or four bud eyes.

## HYBRID CHINA, HYBRID BOURBON, HYBRID NOISETTE
- Vigorous shrub roses with long canes
- Suitable for training onto fences, or wrapping around pillars.
- As freestanding shrubs will create a mound.

After blooming, remove some old wood to make room for new growth, but best to do most of the pruning in the autumn. Some old blooms may need to be shaken off or trimmed. Do not prune too much of hip producers during the season to preserve the hip display for autumn and winter. In autumn, shorten all canes to various lengths to eliminate crossing and rubbing; trim back all side shoots to three or four bud eyes. Re-train to pillars or structures during winter.

## SHRUB
- Shrubs of all sizes
- Upright and spreading habit

Warm climates: strip in January; start pruning in February. During winter or at the end of the dormancy period, remove damage and deadwood, remove one third of old wood, and shorten remaining canes to random lengths. During the season, allow for hips to develop

## RAMBLERS

- Many long, very pliable canes annually from the base of the plant as well as from points along the older canes
- If trained to structures, will grow very tall and wide
- As free standing shrubs will create a huge mound

After bloom, remove old wood (canes that bore blooms) unless the rose is a hip producer. Then save the old blooming wood for a hip display. In late winter, remove deadwood and clutter along with faded hips. Re-train to structures after pruning or during winter

## LARGE-FLOWERED CLIMBING ROSES

- Long canes, some more pliable than others
- Trained to a sturdy structure, some varieties easily cover fifteen to 20 feet.
- If left as a freestanding shrub, they have a mounding habit of six to 8 feet high.
- Non-hip producing—after blooming, remove enough old wood to make room for new
- Hip producers—leave as much old wood as possible; prune old wood in winter
- Re-train to structure
- Shorten all shoots that bore flowers to two or three bud eyes

## EVER-BLOOMING ROSES

*Species*: *Rosa rugosa* and *Rosa rugosa* hybrids
*Habit*: Upright, slightly spreading habit of medium height, with a tendency to sucker freely.

- *Rosa rugosa* and hybrids can be pruned at any time.
- *Rosa rugosa* can be pruned to the ground annually, either at the end of autumn or after the first flush of bloom – if this suits your garden, or treat like the hybrids
- *Rosa rugosa* hybrids should be thinned of older wood at any time of the year, to make room for new growth; remove old wood and crossing branches; trim to desired height in spring.
- If you are growing these roses for hips, do not prune after blooming; instead thin out during winter after the hips have rotted or fallen

## ROSA MOSCHATA

- Tall growing shrub—at times an arching shrub—that can be espaliered or trained to a fence
- As a freestanding shrub, this is more upright than mounding

Prune *Rosa moschata* and its varieties in late winter or spring, after danger of frost has passed. Remove crossing branches. Remove some old wood to create room for new growth. Trim to desired height.

## CHINA

- Varies from short and scrappy to robust and scrappy
- Very twiggy
- There are several vigorous climbing varieties

In warm climates, begin pruning in late winter. Between peaks of bloom, thin out old and dead wood to keep a nice shape. Trim to keep the rose in scale with your garden. In cold climates, wait until danger of frost has passed, then remove dead wood.

## TEA

- Upright, spreading, vigorous
- There are also vigorous climbing varieties

In warm climates, begin pruning in late winter. Between peaks of bloom, thin out old wood and dead wood to keep a nice shape. Trim to keep the rose in scale with your garden. In cold climates, wait until danger of frost has passed, then remove dead wood.

## NOISETTE

- Climbers and vigorous shrubs

In warm climates, begin pruning in late winter. Between peaks of bloom, thin out old and dead wood to keep a nice shape. Trim to keep the rose in scale with your garden. In cold climates, wait until danger of frost has passed, then remove dead wood.

## BOURBON

- Climbing, arching, and compact habits.

At the end of winter or during dormancy, prune to shape, removing twiggy growth, crossing branches, and dead wood. Remove old wood during the season to make room for new growth.

Knock off faded blooms during the season. During the season shorten blooming shoots to strong bud eyes.

## PORTLAND (DAMASK PERPETUAL)
- Shrubby, upright
- There are a few varieties with a vigorous spreading habit

In early spring, shorten all twiggy growth; remove clutter and dead wood. Cut tips of all canes. Deadhead during the season to promote re-bloom by shortening blooming shoots to strong bud eyes.

## MOSS
- Short to medium height; upright, some spreading

After bloom, deadhead and shorten flowering shoot to two or three bud eyes. Remove some old wood to make room for new growth. During winter, shorten all canes to various lengths to eliminate crossing and rubbing; trim back all side shoots to three or four bud eyes.

## HYBRID PERPETUAL
- Medium upright to very tall with a lanky habit.
- Some of these could be trained as climbing plants for pillars or fences.

In early spring, shorten all lateral growths to three or four bud eyes, trim a few inches off all long canes, remove dead wood and twiggy growth, and remove clutter. During the growing season, deadhead faded blooms, remove old growth to make room for new, and trim to fit design.

During the season, between blooming cycles, shorten all shoots that bore flowers to two or three bud eyes

## HYBRID TEA
- Upright plants; rather stiff in habit
- Range from short to very tall shrubs

Warm climates: strip in January. Remove dead, one-third of old wood, and shorten remaining canes by half. Do not leave thin canes. During the growing season, deadhead faded blooms and remove old wood to make room for new growth. When deadheading, shorten all blooming wood to at least five leaflets

## FLORIBUNDA
- Upright; often wider than tall
- Range from very short to very tall

Warm climates: strip in January. At the end of the dormancy period, remove winter damage, remove one-third of old wood, and shorten remaining canes to random lengths. Twiggy canes are acceptable if they are free of clutter. During the growing season, deadhead faded blooms and remove old wood to make room for new growth.

## GRANDIFLORA

• Upright; wide and tall shrubs

Warm climates: strip in January; start pruning in February. At the end of the dormancy period, remove winter damage, remove one third of old wood, and shorten remaining canes to random lengths. During the season, deadhead faded blooms and remove old wood to make room for new growth.

## POLYANTHA

• Short upright shrubs
• There are climbing sports of these roses as well.

Warm climates: strip in January; start pruning in February. At the end of the dormancy period Remove winter damage, remove one third of old wood, and shorten remaining canes by half. Most canes will be thin, remove clutter. During the season, deadhead faded blooms and remove old wood to make room for new growth.

## SHRUB (MEIDILAND, FLOWER CARPET, CAREFREE SERIES, ENGLISH, HYBRID MUSK)

• Shrubs of all sizes
• Upright and spreading habit
• Warm climates: strip in January; start pruning in February

During winter or at the end of the dormancy period, remove damage and deadwood, remove one third of old wood, and shorten remaining canes to random lengths.

During the season, deadhead faded blooms and remove old wood to make room for new growth.

## MINIATURE

• Most average from 6 inches to 18 inches in height
• Upright
• There are climbing forms as well

Shorten to desired height. Remove clutter and deadwood. All canes are thin. Climbing varieties should be pruned in the same manner as large-flowered climbers.

## LARGE-FLOWERED CLIMBER

• Long canes, some more pliable than others
• Trained to a sturdy structure, some varieties easily cover fifteen to 20 feet.
• If left as a freestanding shrub, they have a mounding habit of 6 to 8 feet high.

Warm climates: strip in January; start pruning in February. During dormant period, shorten all branches that are shorter than arm's length to three or four bud eyes, trim tips of all long branches, remove clutter and dead wood, and remove $1/3$ of old wood to make room for new growth. During growing season, deadhead all faded blooms and shorten all canes in the same manner as spring pruning, remove old wood to make room for new growth, and remove clutter.

# INDEX

nurseries, rose, 10-11, 12-15, 16, 17, 18, 60,
83-84, 137, 157, 178
nutrients, plant, 54-55, 76-77

'Oeillet Flamand', 121
'Oklahoma', 46
'Old Blush', 70, 71
old garden roses, 26, 27, 32-33, 43-45, 58,
69-70, 70-72, 105-106, 122, 145, 152, 166
pests of, 33
pruning of, 30-32, 33-34, 44-45, 69-70,
70-72, 106-107, 152
'Old Red Moss', 33
once-blooming roses, 26, 29, 30, 33-34, 95,
105-106, 121
'Ophelia', 117
'Orchid Jubilee', 146
organic fertilizers, 55-57, 76-77
foliar feeding with, 89
at planting time, 64, 66
organic mulches, 79-80
organice pesticides, *see* pesticides, organic
'Othello', 121
own-root roses, 11, 15-18, 68, 170
shipping of, 17-18

parasitic wasps, 88
'Paul Neyron', 121
'Peace', 28, 46, 136
'Peaudouce', 121, 133
pegging of roses, *44*, 44-45, 72
'Peggy Ann Landon', 23
'Perle d'Or', 134
perlite, 158, 177
pesticides, chemical, 34, 50, 86, 112, 113,
115-116, 129-130, 153-154
pesticides, organic, 86, 89, 97, 129-130, 153-154
neem oil as, 82, 86, 89, 97, 99, 100, 101,
113, 116, 129
pyrethrum as, 97, 99, 116, 129
rotenone as, 73, 99, 101, 129
ryania as, 130
sabadilla as, 129
pests, 12, 33, 52-53, 73, 86-88, *87*, 89, 96-101,
*98*, 102, 111, 114-116, 126, 140-141,
153-154
air circulation and, 112
petals, browning of, 96-97
pillars, 20, 138, 143, 144, 149-151, *150*,
152, 161
roses for, 151, 152
types of 150
pine chips, 80
'Pink Princess', 121
*Plant Disease Handbook, The* (Westcott), 69n
plant lice, *see* aphids
polyantha roses, 49, 134
pruning of, 123
spacing of, 67, 140
Portland roses, 43, 44, 45, 58, 107
potted (containerized) roses, 145-149
buying of, at nurseries, 83-84

fertilizing of, 147
insulation of, 176
planting of, in garden, 67, *85*, 86
plantings of, in containers, 148, 149
shipping of, 17-18, 60-61, 148
tree roses as, *147*, 148-149
watering of, 146-147
winter protection for, 175-177
powdery mildew, 50, 82, 134-135, *135*
conditions favoring, 134
controlling of, 135-136
Prairie Rose (*Rosa setigera*), 9, 108, 145, 179
'Prairie Princess', 172
praying mantis, 53
prickles, rose, 13, 30, 35, *92*, *165*
'Princess de Nassau', 71
propagation, 11-17, *17*, 103
'Prosperity', 121
'Prospero', 121
pruners, 24, 30, 156
pruning, 23-34, 41-43, *42*, 49-51, 167
black spot and, 113, 123
as "health" care, 50, 52, 91, 122-123, 135
of modern roses, 30-32, *42*, 46-47, 49,
105-106, 123
of old garden roses, 30-32, 33-34, *42*,
44-45, 69-70, 70-72, 106-107, 152
of once-blooming roses, 26, 29, 30, 33-34,
95, 105-106, 121
of ramblers, 109-111
rejuvenation and, 123
of species roses, 32
tools for, 20, 24, 30-31, 156
in warm climates, 21, 25, 34, 124, 136, 168
pruning saws, 30
'Purple Pavement', 160
pyramids, 39-40
pyrethroids, pyrethrum, 97, 99, 116, 129

'Queen Elizabeth', 47, 97

rabbits, 154
raised beds, 159-161
ground cover roses, 160
soils and, 160, 161
styles of, 160
*see also* rose beds
ramblers, 108-111, 133
powdery mildew and, 135
pruning of, 109-111
training of, 109, 110, *110*, 111,
141-143, *142*
'Red Cascade', 149
'Red Meidiland', 120
'Redwing', 165
repeat-blooming roses, *see* everblooming roses
repellents, animal, 90, 154
'Rhonda', 121
root gall, 126, 156
root rot, 126-127, 156
roots, root systems, 125-126
rootstocks, 14, 15, 16, *48*, 69, 84, 103

*see also* suckering, suckers
*Rosa arkansana*, 9, 145, 165
*Rosa bracteata*, 165
*Rosa canina*, 12, 124, 165
*Rosa carolina*, 75, 124, 145
*Rosa davurica*, 9, 33
*Rosa eglanteria*, 72
*Rosa glauca*, 9
*Rosa moschata*, 183
*Rosa multiflora*, 12, 14, 121, 124
*Rosa palustris*, 62
*Rosa roxburghii*, 164
*Rosa rubiginosa*, 72
*Rosa rugosa*, 32, 127, 165, 174, 182
*Rosa sericea*, 165
*Rosa setigera*, 108, 113, 145, 165
*Rosa spinosissima*, 93, 165
*Rosa virginiana*, 145, 154, 163, 165
*Rosa wichurana*, 121
*Rosa × micrugosa*, 165
rose beds, 137-141
    designs of, 138
    estimating plants for, 139
    grouping of plants in, 139-140, *139*
    sites for,140, 141
    spacing in, 140
    stepping into, 137-138
    tripods in, 138
    *see* also rose gardens
rose cane borer, 52-53
rose chafer, 100
rose curculio, 116
'Rose de Rescht', 43, 107, 121
'Rose du Roi', 43
rose gardens:
    August doldrums in, 117-122
    beds in, 137-141
    companion plantings in, 128, 135
    in late autumn, 162-166
    structures in, 20, 21, 35
    visiting of, 122
    in winter, 9-10, 26
rose leafhopper, 73
rose midge, 114-116
rose mosaic virus, 68-69
roses:
    air curculation and, 112, 136, 140
    anatomy of, 93-94, *92*
    arbors, 164
    autumn planting of, 157-159
    bare-root, *see* bare-root roses
    budded, *see* budded roses
    burying of, 171, 172, 174, 176
    canes (stems), 9-10, 24-25, 50-51, 52, 124, 142-144, *142, 150*-151
    classes of 26-30, 32-33, 58, 151-152
    climate and, size of, 67-68
    climbing, *see* climbing roses
    containerized, *see* potted roses
    cutting of, 91-94, *92*
    deadheading of, 93, 94-95, *95*, 96, *106*, 107, 118, *118*, 134, 137

diseases of, *see* diseases of roses
everblooming, 26, 27, 30, 43, 49, 95, 100, 133, 139
fertilizing of, *see* fertilizers, fertilizing
foliage of, 122
foliar feeding of, 89, 128
as ground cover, 149, 160
growing of, indoors, 176-179
grown on pillars, 149-152, *150, 152*
growth habits of, 121-122
hips, 9, 10, 26-27, 33, 95, 127-128, *128*, 133, 145, 164-165
ice storms and, 167
light requirements of, 61, 177
miniature, *see* miniature roses
modern, *see* modern roses
mulching (mounding) of, 168-170
nurseries, 10-11, 12-15, 16, 17, 18, 60, 83-84, 137, 157, 178
old garden, *see* old garden roses
once-blooming, 26, 29, 30, 33-34, 95, 105-106, 121
ordering of, 10-12, 137
own-root, 11, 15-18, 68, 170
pegging of, *44*, 44-45, 72
pests of, *see* pests
on pillars, 151, 152
planting of, 59-67, 79, 86
plantings of, *see* deer deterrents, 40
potted, *see* potted roses
prickles of, 13, 30, 35, 92, 165
propagation of, 11-17, *17*, 103
pruning of, *see* pruning
in raised beds, 159-161
rejuvenation of, 123
root systems of, 125-126
rustling, 103, 104
shipping of, 17-19, 60-61, 148
shows, 102
shrub, *see* shrub roses
sites for planting of, 62-63
spacing of, 67, 140
species, 12, 32-33, 73, 145
training of, *see* training of roses
transplanting of, 155-157
tree form of, *48*, 148-149
tree roots vs. roots of, 63
viruses, 15, 16, 68-69
watering of, *see* watering
winter protection of, 22, 169-177, *173, 175*
rose scale, 33, 52, 87
rose slugs, 101
rose societies, 10, 20, 23
rose soil sickness, 141
rose stem girdlers, 33, 129
rotenone, 99, 101, 129
'Roundelay', 133
rust, 50, 151-152
ryania, 130

sabadilla, 129
'Sadlers Wells', 121